Dominican Republic

Sarah Cameron

Credits

Footprint credits
Editor: Stephanie Rebello
Production and layout: Emma Bryers
Maps: Kevin Feeney
Cover: Pepi Bluck

Publisher: Patrick Dawson
Managing Editor: Felicity Laughton
Advertising: Elizabeth Taylor
Sales and marketing: Kirsty Holmes

Photography credits
Front cover: Mightyweed/Dreamstime
Back cover: fototehnik/shutterstock

Printed and bound in the United States
of America

Every effort has been made to ensure that
the facts in this guidebook are accurate.
However, travellers should still obtain advice
from consulates, airlines, etc, about travel
and visa requirements before travelling.
The authors and publishers cannot accept
responsibility for any loss, injury or
inconvenience however caused.

Publishing information
Footprint *Focus Dominican Republic*
1st edition
© Footprint Handbooks Ltd
August 2013

ISBN: 978 1 909268 30 2
CIP DATA: A catalogue record for this book
is available from the British Library

® Footprint Handbooks and the Footprint
mark are a registered trademark of
Footprint Handbooks Ltd

Published by Footprint
6 Riverside Court
Lower Bristol Road
Bath BA2 3DZ, UK
T +44 (0)1225 469141
F +44 (0)1225 469461
footprinttravelguides.com

Distributed in the USA by Globe Pequot
Press, Guilford, Connecticut

The content of Footprint *Focus Dominican
Republic* is based on Footprint's *Caribbean
Islands Handbook*, which was researched
and written by Sarah Cameron.

Contents

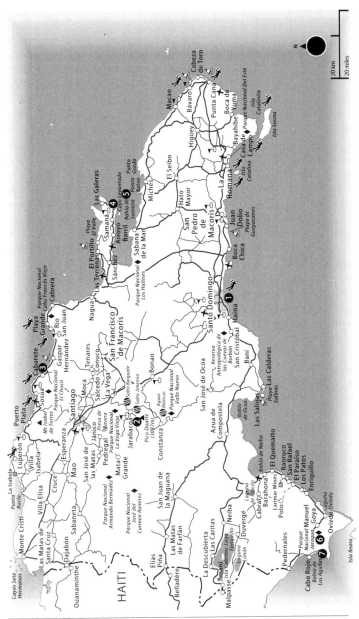

The Dominican Republic is one of the most diverse countries in the Caribbean. You can laze on the beach under swaying palm trees with the blue sea lapping at your toes and sip rum cocktails. Or you can don a wet suit and tackle the rapids on rushing mountain rivers. You can leap off waterfalls, hike up the highest mountain in the West Indies, or cycle the country paths and tracks. National parks protect a range of ecosystems, from subtropical dry forest to cloud forest, home to many birds and other wildlife. If you tire of natural wonders, there are plenty of historical sites to investigate. In addition to Spanish colonial buildings, there are Taíno archaeological sites and cave drawings dating from well before Columbus set foot on the island declaring it to be the most beautiful he had ever seen.

Dominicans are Spanish speaking and Catholic, but their music and rhythms and the way in which they interpret their religion owe a huge debt to the African slaves imported in colonial times to work the sugar plantations and ranches. Their culture is overwhelmingly Latin, with African and American influences, but there is still a romantic attachment to the noble Indian and many Taíno names remain. The legacy of many races and faiths imported into the Spanish colonial society has been to produce some spectacular festivals, particularly the pre-Lenten Carnival. Parades burst with ingenuity and spontaneity within a framework of legends handed down for generations. Each town has a variation on the carnival theme, with the piglet representing the devil in Santiago, the bulls in Monte Cristi and elaborate devil masks in La Vega. Never ones to miss the opportunity for a party, Dominicans also celebrate the Catholic feasts, with each town having its own saint's day. These usually involve the statue of the saint being paraded through the streets accompanied by an incoherent brass band, before returning it to the church for religious services. At fiesta time the rum flows, the band strikes up and everyone hits the dance floor. Merengue and the slower bachata are the local products, but you will hear other Latin styles too, such as salsa.

Planning your trip

Best time to visit the Dominican Republic

This is a tropical island in the sun, where you can expect hot, sunny days and warm, balmy nights, but you can be lucky or unlucky with the weather at any time of year. The dry season is traditionally December-May, but the climate is changing world wide and there is no guarantee that the dry season will be dry nor that the rainy season will be wet. The temperature averages a comfortable 25°C and there is not much seasonal variation, but humidity levels vary. Hurricane season is technically June-November, but two thirds of hurricanes have hit the island in September. Even in winter, which is supposed to be the dry season, the northern parts of the island can be affected by cold fronts moving down from the North American continent; these often bring heavy rain, grey skies and squally northern winds.

You might like to arrange a trip to coincide with an event, rather than a season. At the beginning of the year, the main religious festival is on 21 January, the day of the Virgen de la Altagracia, whale watching is in January-March and Carnival is in February. At Easter all the Dominicans go on holiday, mostly to the beach, so get hotel bookings in early as everywhere is packed. June is the month for windsurfers and kiteboarders, when international competitions are held in Cabarete, while July is good for music lovers with the Santo Domingo Merengue Festival. If baseball is your sport – and it certainly fires up Dominicans – you can catch a game during the season in October-December, or during the Serie Final in January.

Getting to the Dominican Republic

Air
The main gateways are **Punta Cana** (PUJ, www.puntacanainternationalairport.com), **Santo Domingo** (Las Américas, SDQ), **Puerto Plata** (Gregorio Luperón, POP), **La Romana** (LRM), **Samaná** (Juan Bosch, AZS) and **Santiago** (del Cibao, STI). Punta Cana and La Romana are worth flying to if you are staying at one of the all-inclusive hotels along the eastern coast. If you want to start your travels on the south coast, including the capital, then fly to Santo Domingo. For the north coast use the airport outside Puerto Plata. The new international airport at El Catey on the Samaná Peninsula has improved access to Las Terrenas and Samaná.

Some 44 airlines fly to Punta Cana and 52 to Santo Domingo, including **American Airlines** ① www.aa.com, **British Airways** ① www.ba.com, **Air France** ① www.airfrance.com, **US Airways** ① www.usairways.com, **Air Transat** ① www.airtransat.com, **Air Europa** ① www.aireuropa.com, **Air Canada** ① www.aircanada.com, **Delta** ① www.delta.com and **Jet Blue** ① www.jetblue.com, as well as many regional airlines such as **LIAT** ① www.liatairline.com, and **Copa** ① www.copaair.com.

Boat
Several passenger cruise lines from the USA, Canada and Europe call at the Dominican Republic on their Caribbean itineraries, the main stops being at Santo Domingo, La Romana, Samaná and Puerto Plata. **Caribbean Fantasy (American Cruise Ferries)** ①*in Santo Domingo, reservations through Colonial Tours & Travel, T809-688 5285, www.colonialtours.com.do/ferries/ferriesCaribe.htm; in Puerto Rico, T787-832 4800 in*

Mayagüez, T787-725 2643 in San Juan, is a car and passenger overnight ferry between the Dominican Republic and Puerto Rico, with a capacity for 70 vehicles and 1100 passengers, departs 1900, arrives 0800, twice a week between Santo Domingo and San Juan, US$209 return, once a week between Santo Domingo and Mayagüez, US$186 return.

By yacht You must enter at a *puerto habilitado*, a port where there are immigration, customs and coast guard officials, between 0800-1700. These include Santo Domingo, Luperón, Puerto Plata, Samaná, Casa de Campo, Punta Cana, Cap Cana, Las Salinas, Boca Chica.

Boat documents You must show your boat registration and documents received from the captain's port of origin, a list of passengers aboard and their passport numbers, immigration fees of US$43 for the yacht and tourist cards of US$10 per passenger. Thirty days' immigration clearance. The coast guard (Marina Guerra) and other officials will come on board; it is illegal to land before clearance. You will need a coast guard *despacho* to move from port to port, for which it is customary to tip, although it is free of charge.

Transport in the Dominican Republic

Air

There are several domestic airports as well as the international ones listed above: **Dr Joaquín Balaguer**, at El Higuero/La Isabela, Santo Domingo, **Arroyo Barril** and **El Portillo**, Samaná, **Constanza**, **Dajabón**, **Cabo Rojo**, Pedernales, **Osvaldo Virgil**, Monte Cristi, **Cueva Las Maravillas**, San Pedro de Macorís and **María Montéz**, Barahona, T809-524 4144. Some are little more than landing strips, while technically the Barahona airport has international status. Several companies offer internal air taxi or charter services, all based at Dr Joaquín Balaguer International Airport at Higuero/La Isabela, Santo Domingo, including: **Aerolíneas Mas** (www.aerolineasmas.com), **Air Century** (www.aircentury.com), **PAWA Dominicana** (www.pawad.com.do), **Aerodomca** (www.fly-aerodomca.com) and **Dominican Shuttles** (www.dominicanshuttles.com), which has scheduled, charter and shuttle flights and land transfers.

Road

Bus Services between most towns are efficient and inexpensive. In rural areas it can be easy to find a *guagua* (minibus or pick-up) but they are usually filled to the point where you cannot move your legs and luggage is an uncomfortable inconvenience. There are also cars (*carros públicos* or *conchos*) on some of these routes, which are equally dilapidated and crowded. It is possible to buy an extra seat in a *carro* or *guagua* to make yourself more comfortable, or you can hire the whole car to yourself, when it is called a *carrera* and the price is negotiable. Long-distance bus services are very good, with a wide network and several different companies. The three most comfortable and reliable are **Metro**, **Caribe Tours** and **Terrabús**.

Car A valid driving licence from your country of origin or an international licence is accepted for three months. Dominicans drive on the right. Road signs are very poor: a detailed map is essential, plus a knowledge of Spanish for asking directions. Expect to be stopped by the police at the entrance to and exit from towns (normally brief and courteous), at junctions in towns, or any speed-restricted area. Most police or military posts have 'sleeping policemen', speed humps, usually unmarked, outside them. In towns there are often 'ditches' at road junctions, which need as much care as the humps at the entrance and exit to town. Minor roads and many city streets are in poor condition with lots of potholes. At night look out for poorly lighted, or lightless vehicles. Many *motoconchos* have no lights.

The Autopista Duarte is a good, four-lane highway between Santo Domingo and Santiago, but dangerous. It is used by bicycles and horse-drawn carts as well as motorized vehicles, while drivers switch from one lane to the other without warning. Lots of shopping opportunities by the roadside contribute to the hazards, with vehicles swerving on and off the road. Heading east out of Santo Domingo, the Autopista Las Américas goes past the airport (toll RD$30/US$0.75), before becoming the **Autovía del Este**, an excellent road out to La Romana, from where the new Coral Highway runs to Punta Cana. A new toll road north from the Autopista Las Américas to the Catey airport and from there to Las Terrenas on the Samaná Peninsula has cut driving times dramatically, but it is expensive. There are tolls on all principal roads out of the capital: RD$30 (US$0.75), exact change needed. The toll (*peaje*) is paid once for a round trip. Tolls on other roads are variable. On the new road to Catey airport you pay RD$50 (US$1.25) at Peaje Marbella, RD$161 (US$4) at Peaje Naranjal and RD$190 (US$4.75) at Peaje Guaraguao, then from the airport to Las Terrenas you pay RD$450 (US$11.25). On the Coral Highway there is a RD$50 (US$1.25) charge at Peaje Batey La Ceja and another of RD$100 (US$2.50) before Verón. The speed limit for city driving is 40 kmph, for suburban areas 60 kmph and on main roads 80 kmph, although the Autopista Duarte and the Coral Highway are 100 kmph. Speed restrictions on the highways are enforced by police patrols. Service stations generally close at 1800, although there are now some offering 24-hour service. Gasoline prices are around US$5.75 per US gallon for super unleaded, US$5 for diesel.

If driving to Haiti you must get a vehicle permit at the Foreign Ministry (T809-533 1424). Hire cars are not allowed across the border. The drive from Santo Domingo to Port-au-Prince takes about 6 hrs. Buy gourdes from money changers outside the embassy, or at the border, but no more than US$50-worth, rates are much better in Haiti. Also take US$25 for border taxes, which have to be paid in dollars cash.

Car hire Avoid the cheapest companies because their vehicles are not usually trustworthy. Prices for small vehicles start at US$50 per day but can be as much as

Tramping in the tropics

The Dominican Republic provides ideal conditions for medium-distance walking in the tropics. The scenery is varied, with peasant farms, fruit trees, rain forests and high mountains. Mountain streams and waterfalls are perfect for cooling off. The sea is never very far away and affords lovely views from a hill top. Road transport, accommodation, restaurants and rum shops are all within convenient reach but the illusion of remoteness can sometimes be complete. The country possesses the two highest peaks in the Caribbean: Pico Duarte (3087 m) and La Pelona (3082 m), side by side in the Cordillera Central. Hiking up Pico Duarte is now a major attraction with several thousand people making the ascent each year. Although most start from the Park entrance at La Ciénaga, there are other, longer routes you can take. It is important to remember that there is a fee to enter any national park in the Republic and you must always be accompanied by a guide. This is principally to avoid getting lost, a frequent occurrence before the ruling was introduced. Your guide will also ensure that you have enough food and water for your trip and will bring mules to carry your bags and the provisions. The guides are well trained and highly experienced, but they only speak Spanish, so you are advised to learn some if you want to communicate. Take plenty of high-factor sun screen and a wide-brimmed hat. You may feel cool up in the mountains, but the sun burns just as much as at lower altitude. Rain comes in intense bursts or pours hard all day, so waterproof clothing is not much use, but a small collapsible umbrella can be useful against showers or the sun. Good footwear is important as you will be tramping over rough terrain and often through rivers. Walking sticks are advised, particularly if it has been raining and the tracks are slippery or muddy. You need to carry plenty of water. Do not drink from the rivers unless you have a purification system with you.

US$90. Weekly rates are better value. Credit cards are widely accepted; the cash deposit is normally twice the sum of the contract. The minimum age for hiring a car is usually 25, although some companies will rent to 20 year olds; maximum period for driving is 90 days. Mopeds and motorcycles are everywhere and are very noisy. Most beach resorts hire motorcycles for US$15-35 a day. By law, the driver of a motorcycle must wear a crash helmet; passengers are not required to wear one.

Cycling The Dominican Republic has miles of dirt roads and endless mule trails, making it a paradise for mountain bikers. There is also some good road biking if you don't mind sharing the roads with trucks, mules, motorbikes and *guaguas*. There are hundreds of great rides in the mountains and along coastal routes. These can change after hurricanes and rain storms. You can bike all year round. It is hottest from 1200-1500, so if you want to cover large distances get an early start and take a long lunch break. In the mountains it is hot during the day, but gets cool at night, so dressing in layers and having warm clothing for after sunset is important. Good rain gear is also recommended. Carry at least two water bottles and make sure you drink more than you think you need. There are only a few places to rent mountain bikes, including **Iguana Mama** based in Cabarete, **Rancho Baiguate** in Jarabacoa and **Hotel El Morro** in Montecristi. Sometimes some of the local bike shops have bikes to rent. Equipment at hotels is often not well maintained; this doesn't mean that they are not great bikes for a coastal cruise, but anyone wanting a real mountain bike adventure should not be fooled into thinking that they have a suitable bike at their hotel.

Taxi There are taxis at airports and major hotels, or you can call a radio taxi listed in the telephone directory. If travelling by private taxi, bargaining is very important. Motorcyclists (*motoconchos*) also offer a taxi service and take several passengers on pillion. In some towns, eg Samaná, *motoconchos* and cyclists pull four-seater covered rickshaws. During the day a short distance costs US$0.50 for one passenger. For longer journeys negotiate fare first. During the night fares double. There are usually fixed *público* rates between cities, so inquire first. They can take two passengers in front and four on the back seat, regardless of the size of the car, so the ride is often uncomfortable, but friendly.

Where to stay in the Dominican Republic

There is a wide range of accommodation, from the four- or five-star, all-inclusive beach resorts run by international companies, to simple lodgings for local travelling salesmen. The cheaper all-inclusive hotels usually offer buffet food and local alcoholic drinks (rum and beer), which can get boring after a few days, while the more expensive ones offer à la carte restaurants and wine; you get what you pay for. In Santo Domingo the string of four- or five-star hotels along the Malecón are designed to cater for businessmen, diplomats and politicians and are of international standard, with business centres, elegant restaurants, casinos, vibrant nightlife and conference centres. Most hotels charge 26% tax and service on top of room rates. There are plenty of nice places to stay in the **$$$** range, which offer peace and quiet, good food and comfortable rooms in pleasant locations. There are several delightful small hotels in the colonial city in renovated old mansions with bags of character. In more modest guesthouses, a weekly or monthly rate, with discount, can be arranged. Hotels with rooms for less than US$30 will be basic with erratic plumbing and electricity; check the lock on the door.

Food and drink in the Dominican Republic

Food
Like most Caribbean cooking, local food tends to be calorific. The usual starches, rice, yams and plantains, underpin most meals, while chips/fries are usually also available. Dominicans like their food well seasoned, so sauces include a good deal of garlic, pepper and oregano. They also add a lot of salt and hot pepper sauce to their plate of food. The staple of *comida criolla* (Creole cooking) is the dish known as *bandera dominicana* (the Dominican flag), a colourful arrangement of stewed beef, rice, plantains and red beans, which can be rather bland. More exotic and challenging is the legendary *sancocho* or *salcocho prieto*, a hearty stew made of six or seven different types of meat as well as vegetables. Dominican breakfasts can be a serious affair. The dish *mangú* is mashed plantain, drizzled with oil and accompanied by fried onions, usually served with eggs, deep fried cheese and sausage or bacon. Goat meat is a great favourite and usually comes either as roast (*chivo asado*) or stewed (*chivo guisado*). A *locrio* is a rice dish, accompanied by meat, chicken or sausages, and the formidable *mondongo* is a tripe stew. Another local speciality is the *asopao*, somewhere between a soup and a pilau-style rice dish (sometimes unappetizingly translated as soupy rice) that is served with fish, shrimp or chicken. The

Price codes

Where to stay

$$$$ over US$150 $$$ US$66-150
$$ US$30-65 $ under US$30
Price of a double room in high season, including taxes.

Restaurants

$$$ over US$12 $$ US$7-12 $ US$6 and under
Prices for a two-course meal for one person, excluding drinks or service charge.

ubiquitous street snacks such as *pastelitos* (pasties or turnovers filled with minced beef, chicken or cheese) are fried according to demand, as are *quipes* (cracked-wheat fritters with a meat filling) or *platanitos* (hot plantain crisps). *Tostones*, or twice-fried slices of plantain, are often served as a side dish.

Most Dominican restaurants assume their customers to be carnivorous and the number of vegetarian restaurants is still limited. Fresh fruit is plentiful all year round and changes according to season. *Lechoza* (papaya) is commonly served at breakfast, as is *guineo* (sweet banana), *naranja* (orange), *piña* (pineapple) and mango. More unusual are *jagua* (custard apple), *caimito* and *mamey*. Many *cafeterías* serve delicious fresh smoothies (*batidas*), made out of any of these fruits, water and milk (optional, *con leche*).

Eating out

Lunch is the main meal of the day for most Dominicans. *Comedores*, or diners, serve a variety of local specialities but for best value choose the *menú*, or dish of the day. This is usually meat, rice, beans and some salad or vegetable for around US$4. A restaurant is more upmarket than a *comedor*, serving international-style food in the evenings at higher prices. Eating out is generally not expensive, however, and even in gourmet restaurants you can eat well with a couple of drinks for around US$30 per person.

Drink

Statistics reveal that Dominicans account for one of the world's highest per capita consumptions of alcohol, and a look around any *colmado* (corner store) will confirm this fact. The Presidente brand of lager beer comes in two sizes (*pequeño* or *grande*) and seems to enjoy a near monopoly. Other beers such as Quisqueya and Bohemia are much less visible. *Mamajuana* is a home-made spiced rum mixed with honey and sweet wine, sold in markets and on street corners, frequently called the Dominican viagra. There are many rums (the most popular brands are Barceló, Brugal and Bermúdez). Light rum (*blanco*) is the driest and has the highest proof, usually mixed with fruit juice or other soft drink (*refresco*). Watch out for cocktails mixed with 151° proof rum. Amber (*amarillo*) or gold (*dorado*) is aged at least a year in an oak barrel and has a lower proof and more flavour, while dark rum (*añejo*) is aged for several years and is smooth enough, like a brandy, to be drunk neat or with ice and lime. **Brugal** allows visitors to tour its bottling plant in Puerto Plata, on Avenida Luis Genebra, just before the entrance to the town, and offers free Daiquirí. In a disco, *un servicio* is a half litre bottle of rum with a bucket of ice and *refrescos*. In rural areas this costs US$5-6, but in cities rises to US$15.

Top rum cocktails

There is nothing better at the end of a busy day than finding a pleasant spot overlooking the sea with a rum in your hand to watch the sunset and look out for the green flash. The theory is that the more rum you drink, the more likely you are to see this flash of green on the horizon as the sun goes down.

There are hundreds of different rums in the Caribbean, each island producing the best, of course. The main producers are Jamaica, Cuba, Barbados, Guyana, Martinique and the Dominican Republic, but other islands such as Grenada also produce excellent brands. Generally, the younger, light rums are used in cocktails and aged, dark rums are drunk on the rocks or treated as you might a single malt whisky. Cocktails first became popular after the development of ice-making in the USA in 1870, but boomed in the 1920s partly because of prohibition in the USA and the influx of visitors to Cuba, the Bahamas and other islands, escaping stringent regulations. People have been drowning their rum in cola ever since the Americans brought bottled drinks in to Cuba during the war against Spain at the end of the 19th century, hence the name, Cuba Libre. You can in fact adapt any cocktail recipe to substitute other spirits and incorporate rum. It makes an excellent Bloody Mary, for example.

One of the nicest and most refreshing cocktails is a **Daiquirí**, invented in Santiago de Cuba in 1898 by an engineer in the Daiquirí mines. The natural version combines 1½ tablespoons of sugar, the juice of half a lime, some drops of maraschino liqueur, 1½ oz light dry rum and a lot of shaved ice, all mixed in a blender and then served piled high in a wide, chilled champagne glass with a straw. You can also have fruit versions, with strawberry, banana, peach or pineapple, using fruit or fruit liqueur.

Another Cuban favourite, drinkable at any time of the day or night, is the **Mojito**, once popular with Ernest Hemingway and his friends in Havana. Put half a tablespoon of sugar, the juice of half a lime and some lightly crushed mint leaves in a tall glass. Stir and mix well, then add some soda water, ice cubes, 1½ oz light dry rum and top up with soda water to taste. Garnish with mint leaves and serve with a straw.

Everybody has heard of the old favourite, **Piña Colada**, which can be found on all the islands and is probably the most popular of the fruit-based cocktails. Combine and blend coconut liqueur, pineapple juice, light dry rum and shaved ice, then serve with a straw in a glass, a pineapple or a coconut.

Many Caribbean hotels offer you a welcome cocktail when you stagger out of the taxi, jet-lagged from your transatlantic flight. This is often a watered-down punch, with a poor quality rum and sickly fruit juice. You are more likely to find something palatable in the bar, but it always depends on which blend of juice the barman favours. In Grenada, rum punch is improved enormously with the addition of nutmeg sprinkled on top. The standard recipe for a **Rum Punch** is: 'one of sour, two of sweet, three of strong and four of weak'. If you measure that in fluid ounces, it comes out as 1 oz of lime juice, 2 oz of syrup (equal amounts of sugar and water, boiled for a few minutes), 3 oz of rum and 4 oz of water, fruit juices, ginger ale, or whatever takes your fancy. You could add ice and a dash of Angostura Bitters from Trinidad, use nutmeg syrup from Grenada or Falernum from Barbados instead of sugar syrup, and garnish it with a slice of lime. Delicious.

Despite being a major coffee-producer, the country does not always offer visitors good coffee, and much of what is served in hotels is either American-style watery instant or over-stewed and over-strong. Good coffee is available in small *comedores*, *cafeterías* and even from street vendors, who sell a small, dark shot for a few pesos. **Santo Domingo** is the mainstream brand, **Monte Alto** comes in *especial* or *orgánico* (their factory can be toured in Jarabacoa), and there are several single estate coffees worth trying if you can find them. Thick hot chocolate is traditionally drunk for breakfast and, although local chocolate is nothing special, Dominican cocoa is high quality and a major export, much of it organic.

Festivals in the Dominican Republic

Each town's saint's day is celebrated with several days of festivities known as *patronales*.

1 Jan New Year is celebrated in the capital on Av Francisco Alberto Caamaño Deñó (formerly Av del Puerto) beside the river. The major bands and orchestras of the country give a free concert, which attracts thousands of people. The celebration ends with fireworks and the whole area becomes a huge disco.

6 Jan Epiphany.

21 Jan Day of the **Virgen de la Altagracia**, spiritual mother of the Dominicans, is celebrated with *velaciones*, or night-long vigils, and African-influenced singing and music, found in many towns. Higüey is the site of a mass pilgrimage and huge all-night party.

26 Jan Duarte Day.

27 Feb Independence Day.

Feb Carnival is notable in Santo Domingo for the parade along the Malecón. Each Sun in Feb there are celebrations in different areas of the city on a rotational basis. Carnival in Santiago de los Caballeros is very colourful; its central character is the piglet, which represents the devil. Celebrations are held on Sat.

On Sun in Feb at Monte Cristi there are the festivals of the Toros versus the Civiles.

La Vega has become so popular for its Carnival that celebrations are now held on Sat and Sun in Feb with elaborate masks worn by participants. There are about 60 groups sponsored by local businesses, each with about 60 members. New costumes are created every year, while the old ones are passed on to other, smaller towns, such as Bonao.

Mar/Apr Holy Week is the most important holiday time for Dominicans, when there are processions and festivities such as the *guloyas* in San Pedro de Macorís, the mystical-religious *ga-ga* in sugar cane villages and the *cachúas* in Cabral in the southwest.

Apr/May Santo Domingo International Book Fair held in the Plaza de la Cultura, with free concerts and other cultural events.

1 May Labour Day.

May/Jun Corpus Christi.

Jul Merengue Festival includes festivals of gastronomy, cocktails and exhibitions of handicrafts and fruit.

16 Aug Restoration Day parades.

24 Sep Our Lady of Las Mercedes.

Last week Sep Sosúa's annual Merengue Festival.

Nov Puerto Plata has an annual Merengue Festival on the Malecón La Puntilla.

25 Dec Christmas Day.

Music and dance

The most popular dance is the merengue, which dominates the musical life of the Dominican Republic and has spread across the water with migrants to colonize New York as well. Merengue is believed to have developed in the mid-19th century as a local version of European dances for couples, such as *contredanse*. An Afro-Caribbean flavour was added with lively rhythms and lyrics to reflect social commentary. It was the music of the people, from cane-cutters to dock workers, but, with regional variants it survived as a sort of folk music. There would be four musicians, playing the *cuatro*, similar to a guitar, the *güira*, a cylindrical scraper of African origin but akin to the Indian gourd scraped with a forked stick, the *tambora*, a double-headed drum using male goatskin played with the hand on one head and female goatskin played with a stick on the other, and the *marimba*, a wooden box with plucked metal keys. Despite the regional variations, the merengue of the Cibao Valley around Santiago developed most strongly and became known as the *merengue típico*. In the 1920s, it was played with an accordion, introduced by the Germans, a *güira*, *tambora* and *marimba*, with the accordion being the most important. Over the years, other instruments have been added, such as the saxophone, horn or electric bass guitar. A merengue would have a short introduction, *paseo*, then move into the song, or merengue, followed by a call and response section, the *jaleo*. Although similar to some Cuban or other Latin music and dance, the steps of the merengue have always been simpler, with a basic two-step pattern, but at a fast tempo with a suggestive hip movement.

The other main music style you will find in the Dominican Republic is bachata, which also emerged from the peasant and shanty town dwellers. It was music for the soul, for the poor and downtrodden, the dispossessed farmers who were forced off the land in the 1960s and flooded into the urban slums with their guitar-based *canciones de amargue*, songs of bitterness. The traditional group had one or two guitars, maracas, bongo and *marimba*, with a solo male singer, who sang songs based on the Cuban *son*, Mexican *ranchera*, merengue and boleros. The songs expressed the frustrations of the newly urban male, a *macho* without a cause, who was often unemployed and often dependent on a woman for his income. The sudden rise in popularity of bachata was principally due to Juan Luis Guerra, who experimented with the romantic, sentimental genre and sensitively created a poetry which appealed to everyone, particularly women. Most bachata songs are similar to boleros, with the guitar, the rhythm and the sentimentality, but faster than usual and with one singer rather than three.

Entertainment in the Dominican Republic

The Dominican Republic comes alive at night, whether it is families taking a promenade along the Malecón in the cool air after dark or youngsters hitting the clubbing scene. Tourists who spent their days lying on the beach move into the bars and discos after dark and many beach bars can be lively both day and night, often with live music and dancing. There is a wide variety of music played, although merengue dominates and gets the hips swaying and the feet tapping. The best clubs are in the capital city, but

Baseball

The national sport is baseball. The Dominican Republic has produced a phenomenal number of great players and the game has become known as a way out of poverty, with thousands of boys hoping to be plucked out of obscurity by team selectors and paid a fortune to play their favourite game. The best players are recruited by US and Canadian teams who maintain feeder academies in the Republic; about half of the 300 professional Dominican players in the USA come from San Pedro de Macorís. The regular season starts on the last Friday in October and runs until the end of December, with national and big league players participating. At the beginning of January for three weeks, round robin semi-final matches are held, after which the two best teams compete in the Serie Final in the last week of January.

there are many great bars in coastal areas, particularly in places like Cabarete, frequented by the windsurfing crowd, and in Las Terrenas. Hotels in Punta Cana also offer a wide range of entertainment with some very popular clubs. Things start to happen around midnight and go on late, usually until around 0400 but often after that. Dominicans visit their local corner store, *colmado*, for a drink, dominoes and a chat in the evenings, but the essentially Dominican nightlife all over the country can be found at the local car wash. Here, massive sound systems are set up, cold beer is brought in and floodlights illuminate the dance floor as couples go through their paces to the latest releases and old favourites. Everyone knows the words to every song, learned from birth, and children can dance as soon as they can stand on two feet. Look out for festivals and saints' days, which usually become huge outdoor street parties, often with live bands playing, sponsored by the beer or rum companies.

Essentials A-Z

Accident and emergency

T911. Politur, the Tourist Police, www.politur.gob.do, has a visible presence in areas of high concentration of tourists. It can be contacted at Calle Las Damas, Santo Domingo, T809-689 6464, and at offices in Baní, Barahona, Bávaro, Bayahibe, Boca Chica, Cabarete, Cabrera, Constanza, Higüey, Jarabacoa, Juan Dolio, La Romana, Las Terrenas, Luperón, Monte Cristi, Palenque, Puerto Plata, Punta Cana, Río San Juan, Samaná, Sánchez, San José de las Matas, Santiago, Sosúa, Uvero Alto and at international airports. If you have anything stolen go to a police station to report the crime and get a signed, stamped declaration for your insurance company.

Dress

Light clothing, preferably cotton, is best all year round. However, if you are going up into the mountains you will need warm clothing for after dark as the temperature can drop to 0°C. In winter on the north coast you may need a cardigan or light fleece in the evenings. Dominicans dress smartly to go out at night, so take something appropriate for formal hotel dining rooms and nightclubs, particularly in Santo Domingo. Shorts are not permitted in the cathedral in Santo Domingo. Swimwear is for the beach only.

Electricity

110 volts, 60 cycles AC current. American-type, flat-pin plugs are used. There are occasional power cuts, so take a torch with you when you go out at night. Many establishments have their own (often noisy) generators.

Embassies and consulates

For a full list of Dominican embassies abroad and foreign embassies and consulates in the Dominican Republic, visit http://embassy.goabroad.com.

Health

See your GP or travel clinic at least 6 weeks before departure for general advice on travel risks and vaccinations. Try phoning a specialist travel clinic if your own doctor is unfamiliar with health conditions in the Dominican Republic. Make sure you have sufficient medical travel insurance, get a dental check, know your own blood group and if you suffer a long-term condition, such as diabetes or epilepsy, obtain a Medic Alert bracelet/necklace (www.medicalert.co.uk). If you wear glasses, take a copy of your prescription.

Vaccinations

You should be up to date with your typhoid, tetanus and polio inoculations. The vaccine against infectious hepatitis is a good idea. Malaria prevention is recommended, as it is present in the southwest and the west of the country. There is also dengue fever: the Aedes mosquito breeds in urban areas and is more prevalent when there has been lots of rain. There is no cure, so prevention is essential. There is rabies, so if you are at high risk get yourself vaccinated before you travel. In any case, if you are bitten seek medical help immediately.

Health risks

The most common cause of travellers' diarrhoea is from eating contaminated food. Be wary of salads (what were they washed in, who handled them), reheated foods or food that has been left out in the sun having been cooked earlier in the day. There is a simple adage that says wash it, peel it, boil it or forget it. It is also standard advice to be careful with water and ice. Bottled water is readily available all over the country; tap water is generally not considered safe to drink. Swimming in sea or river water that has been contaminated by sewage can also be a cause; ask locally if it is safe. Diarrhoea may also be caused by viruses, bacteria (such as E-coli), protozoal (such as giardia), salmonella and cholera. It may be accompanied by vomiting or by severe abdominal pain. Any kind of diarrhoea responds well to the replacement of water and salts. Sachets of rehydration salts can be bought in most pharmacies and can be dissolved in boiled water. If the symptoms persist, consult a doctor.

Mosquitoes are more of a nuisance than a serious hazard but some, of course, are carriers of serious diseases such as malaria or dengue fever, so it is sensible to avoid being bitten as much as possible and use a good insect repellent. Remember that DEET (Di-ethyltoluamide) is the gold standard. Apply the repellent every 4-6 hrs but more often if you are sweating heavily. If a non-DEET product is used, check who tested it. Validated products (tested at the London School of Hygiene and Tropical Medicine) include Mosiguard, Non-DEET Jungle formula and non-DEET Autan. If you want to use citronella remember that it must be applied very frequently (ie hourly) to be effective.

The climate is hot; the Dominican Republic is a tropical country and protection against the sun will be needed. To reduce the risk of sunburn and skin cancer, make sure you pack high-factor sun cream, light-coloured loose clothing and a hat.

If you get sick

Most of the large hotels have medical centres with qualified personnel to assist you, many have a doctor on call. Wherever you are staying, the management can direct you to a doctor or health centre. Facilities in cities and tourist centres are modern and good. If you need to be evacuated abroad for medical treatment, there are charter planes equipped for emergencies. Make sure that you have adequate insurance.

Useful websites

www.bgtha.org British Global and Travel Health Association.

www.cdc.gov Centers for Disease Control and Prevention; US government site that gives excellent advice on travel health and details of disease outbreaks.

www.fco.gov.uk British Foreign and Commonwealth Office travel site has useful information on each country, people, climate and a list of UK embassies/consulates.

www.fitfortravel.scot.nhs.uk A-Z of vaccine/health advice for each country.

www.guiamedica.com.do A directory of all the medical centres, clinics, dentist surgeries and hospitals in the Dominican Republic.

www.sensitivescreening.com/mht.htm Number One Health Group offers travel screening services, vaccine and travel health advice, email/SMS text vaccine reminders and screens returned travellers for tropical diseases.

Language

The official language is Spanish, although English, German, French and Italian are spoken in tourist resorts by guides and some hotel employees. English is the language most commonly taught to tourism workers. If you are planning to travel off the beaten track, a working knowledge of Spanish is recommended. Spanish courses of 1-4 weeks with dance, wind/kite surfing, scuba diving and a cultural programme are offered by Càlédònià – Languages, Culture, Adventure, 33 Sandport St, Edinburgh EH6 6EP, Scotland, T0131-621 7721, www.caledonialanguages.co.uk. Spanish plus dance is offered in the school in Santo Domingo, with evenings out to local dance venues and other cultural activities arranged by the school. The school in Sosua offers Spanish plus dance and wind/kite surfing and diving and is ideally suited to watersports enthusiasts. Homestays or aparthotel accommodation available. Trekking on Pico Duarte and the surrounding area is also organized all year round.

Money
Currency
The Dominican peso (RD$) is the only legal tender. There are coins in circulation of 1, 5, 10 and 25 pesos, and notes of 10, 20, 50, 100, 500, 1000 and 2000 pesos. The peso is divided into 100 centavos, but these are rarely used nowadays.

Exchange
The exchange rate fluctuates against the dollar and was trading at around RD$40=US$1 in Aug 2013. Banks and exchange houses (*casas de cambio*) are authorized to deal in foreign exchange. Cambios often give better rates than banks. Do not rely on the airport bank being open. The US dollar and the euro are the best currencies to bring. Sterling can be changed at **BanReservas**. If stuck at weekends, most hotels will change money; cash only.

Plastic/TCs/banks (ATMs)
Nearly all major hotels, restaurants and stores accept most credit cards. Several banks will give cash against Visa, Mastercard or American Express cards, usually with 5% commission. It is advisable to inform your bank or credit card company before you use your card in the Dominican Republic. Some companies will put a stop on your card after you have used it twice. This is for your own protection as the Dominican Republic has a high rate of credit card fraud. ATMs are an easy way to get cash and you will get close to the market rate, plus a commission of up to 5%. They are sometimes out of action at weekends and holidays. Travellers' cheques should be denominated in US dollars; you may have difficulty changing them other than in Santo Domingo and tourist places. The commercial banks include: **Scotiabank** (Santo Domingo and other cities),

BanReservas, Banco Popular, Banco BHD, Banco del Progreso and others. Money can be sent via **Western Union**, which operates through **Vimenca** but the exchange rate is up to 20% higher than at banks.

Cost of travelling
Compared with much of the rest of the Caribbean, the Dominican Republic is relatively economical to travel around, although it is considerably more expensive than much of Latin America. Cheap places to stay start from about US$25-30 for a double room, but this often requires some negotiation. Santo Domingo has some reasonable hotels and guest houses in this price range for tourists, but outside the city they are usually aimed at Dominicans and can be very basic with a rudimentary level of safety and comfort. For a simple room, clean, comfortable, with a functioning bathroom and a decent breakfast, you should expect to pay US$50-60 a night. Above that you will find rising standards of luxury costing up to four figures for the very best. Eating out can be cheap if you limit yourself to the family-run *comedores*, which serve Dominican meals of meat, rice and beans for US$3-5. However, even in top restaurants you can eat and drink well for US$30. If you are hiring a car, fuel is relatively cheap at less than US$6 a US gallon, but choose your routes carefully as the new toll roads are costly. Long-distance bus travel is still good value, with bus companies charging US$8 for the 2½-hr trip between Santo Domingo and Samaná.

Opening hours
Banks: 0830-1500 Mon-Fri. **Government offices**: 0730-1430. **Offices**: 0830-1230, 1430-1630; some offices and shops work 0930-1730 Mon-Fri, 0800-1300 Sat. **Shops**: normally 0800-1800, some open all day Sat and mornings on Sun and holidays. Large shopping malls stay open until 2100 except Sun when they are open 0900-1800. Most shops in tourist areas stay open through the

siesta and on Sun. Restaurants stay open until 2400 Sun-Thu and until 0200 Fri, Sat and holidays.

Safety
On no account change money on the streets. Banks and cambios offer the market rate and are safer. Be careful with 'helpers' at the airports, who speed your progress through the queues and then charge US$15-20 for their services. Single men have complained of the massive presence of pimps and prostitutes. Be prepared to say 'no' a lot. These problems do not occur in rural areas and small towns, where travellers have been impressed with the open and welcoming nature of the Dominicans. Violent crime against tourists is rare but, as anywhere, watch your money and valuables in cities late at night and on beaches. The streets of Santo Domingo are not considered safe after 2300. Electricity black-outs mean that street lighting is not always efficient. Purse snatchers on motorcycles operate in cities and they may be armed. Keep away from anything to do with illegal drugs. You may be set up and find yourself facing an extended stay in a Dominican prison. Beware of drug-pushers on the Malecón in Santo Domingo and near the Cathedral in Puerto Plata. Carry a photocopy of your passport on you and leave all valuables in the hotel safe.

Tax
Airport departure tax is US$20, but is usually included in the price of your ticket. Hotels add 26% tax and service to your bill. VAT, known as ITBIS, is generally 18%, although products in the basic food basket such as coffee, chocolate and yoghurt are taxed at 8%, rising to 16% in 2016.

Telephone
The main area code is 809- although a few are 829-. Each phone number has 10 digits and if you are only quoted 7, it is usually an 809- number. Most people now have cell phones and there are few public phones. If you wish to purchase a local sim card or phone, the companies offering service are Claro-Codetel, Orange, Tricom and Viva. The latter also sells wireless internet for your laptop. Wi-Fi hot-spots are plentiful.

Time
Atlantic Standard Time, 4 hrs behind GMT, 1 hr ahead of EST.

Tipping
Restaurants add 10% service but diners usually leave more than that, up to an extra 10%. Dominicans do not normally tip taxis. Hotel porters and chambermaids appreciate tips.

Tourist information
The Ministerio de Turismo is at Calle Cayetano Germosén, esq Av Gregorio Luperón, Santo Domingo, T809-221 4660, www.godominicanrepublic.com. There are small tourist offices in most towns, at the airports and cabinas in some tourist spots, such as in the colonial city in Plaza España (T809-686 3858).

Vaccinations
There are no vaccinations demanded by immigration officials in the Dominican Republic. For further details, see Health, page 16.

Visas and immigration
All visitors require a passport. Citizens and residents of the USA, Canada and the majority of EU countries need a US$10 30-day tourist card, usually bought on arrival before lining up in the queue for immigration. You may extend this to 90 days by paying US$20 to immigration on departure. Citizens of Argentina, Chile, Ecuador, Israel, Japan, Peru, South Korea, Uruguay do not need a tourist card or a visa to enter.

Weights and measures

Officially metric, but business is often done on a pound/yard/US gallon basis. Gas stations sell fuel in US gallons. Land areas in cities are measured by square metres, but in the countryside by the *tarea*, one of which equals 624 sq m.

Contents

Footprint features

Dominican Republic

Santo Domingo

Travellers have been marvelling at this city since the beginning of the 16th century, when its streets, fortresses, palaces and churches were the wonder of the Caribbean and *conquistadores* set off from the port on the river to discover new territory for Spain in the Americas. Santo Domingo, the first European city in the Western Hemisphere, is now the capital and business centre of the Dominican Republic. Busy and modern, it sprawls along the Caribbean coast and inland along the banks of the Río Ozama. Restoration of the old city on the west bank of the river has made the area very attractive, with open-air cafés and pleasant squares near the waterfront. Those who have wealth flaunt it by building ostentatious villas and driving German cars, but the slums are some of the worst in the Caribbean.

Arriving in Santo Domingo → *See Getting to the Dominican Republic, page 6, and Transport in the Dominican Republic, page 7, for further information.*

Getting there
Aeropuerto Las Américas, east of Santo Domingo, is the main international airport for the capital, receiving flights from North and South America and Europe. The international ferry from Puerto Rico docks at the mouth of the Río Ozama, beside the Colonial Zone and within walking distance of hotels there. If you have flown to another airport and arrive in Santo Domingo by bus, each bus company has its own terminal, there is no central bus station.

Getting around
The Colonial Zone can be toured on foot, but to travel further afield you will need public transport, in the form of taxis, whether privately hired or shared, buses, *motoconcho*, motor-bike taxis or the Metro. Car hire for travelling around Santo Domingo is not recommended.

Tourist information
There is a tourist information desk at the airport, but it may be closed if you arrive late at night. In Plaza España in the Colonial Zone, there is a cabin, **Punto de Interés Turismo** ① *open 0900-1700*, with information and computers with free internet access for tourists. On Arzobispo Meriño, just along from the main entrance to the Cathedral, are the offices of the **Cluster Turístico de Santo Domingo**, which has tourist information provided by businesses which are members of the Cluster.

Dominican people

African slaves began to arrive in Santo Domingo from the 1530s. Although the proportion of slaves in the colony never matched that of Saint-Domingue, blacks nevertheless formed an important part of the colonial population. As the indigenous Taíno inhabitants were exterminated within half a century of European colonization, African slaves and their descendants became the largest non-European group. From the mixing of Africans and Europeans emerged the mulatto population to which the majority of Dominicans nowadays belong. Successive governments tried to attract non-African settlers, especially after Independence, when fears of Haitian territorial ambitions were at their highest and the 'whitening' of the population was deemed desirable. Some Canarian and Italian migrants took up the offer of government-assisted relocation schemes, while an important community from the Middle East, mostly Syrians but known generically as *turcos*, arrived to establish businesses. Another group of immigrants, known as *cocolos*, left the English-speaking Caribbean islands of Tortola, Anguilla and St Kitts to work in the Republic's sugar plantations. Their descendants still live around San Pedro de Macorís. Under Trujillo, there was even an attempt to settle Japanese farmers near the border with Haiti, presumably as a deterrent to would-be smugglers and rustlers. This racial policy is no longer on the agenda, but it shows how the country's leaders have traditionally viewed the nation as white, Hispanic and Christian.

Conventional demographic surveys suggest that about 15% of Dominicans are white, 15% black and 65% mixed-race or mulatto (the rest being of Middle Eastern or other origins). In spite of the indigenous Taíno population becoming effectively extinct after only 50 years after the arrival of the first European colonists, recent research into DNA in the Dominican Republic and Puerto Rico has shown that claims of Taíno ancestry are not fanciful and that much of the population does indeed carry Amerindian genes passed down by enslaved Taína women.

Background

The first wooden houses were built in 1496 by Christopher Columbus' (Cristóbal Colón) brother Bartolomé on the eastern bank of the Río Ozama after the failure of the settlement at La Isabela on the north coast. In 1498 the Governor, Nicolás de Ovando, moved the city to the other side of the river and started building with stone, a successful move which was continued by Diego Colón, Christopher's son, when he took charge in 1509. It then became the first capital city in Spanish America. For years the city was the base for the Spaniards' exploration and conquest of the continent. Santo Domingo holds the title 'first' for a variety of offices: first city, having the first Audiencia Real, cathedral, university, coinage, etc. In view of this, UNESCO has designated Santo Domingo a World Cultural Heritage Site. However, Santo Domingo's importance waned when Spain set up her colonies in Peru and Mexico with seemingly limitless silver and gold to finance the Crown. Hurricanes managed to sink 15 ships in 1508, 18 in 1509 and many more in later years. 1562 brought an earthquake which destroyed much of the town; 1586 brought Sir Francis Drake, who attacked from inland where defences were vulnerable, looted and pillaged and set the city alight. He was the first of many British and French pirates and privateers who attacked in the 16th and 17th centuries and rebuilding works were continually in progress.

In the 1930s, the dictator Rafael Leonidas Trujillo renamed the city Ciudad Trujillo and embarked on a series of public works. After his assassination in 1961 the city immediately reverted to the title of Santo Domingo, but his successor, Joaquín Balaguer, continued to build on a monumental scale. Prestigious projects such as the Faro a Colón took pride of place over social spending on education, health and housing for the poor. Governments since the 1960s have been criticized for concentrating on the capital and ignoring the provinces. As a result, migration to the capital has surged and little has been done to prevent the growth of slums and poor *barrios*. However, tourism is booming and it is a lively and vibrant place to spend a few days.

Santo Domingo

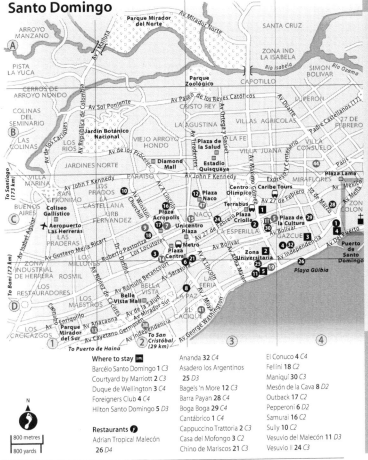

Where to stay 🛏
Barcéló Santo Domingo 1 *C3*
Courtyard by Marriott 2 *C3*
Duque de Wellington 3 *C4*
Foreigners Club 4 *C4*
Hilton Santo Domingo 5 *D3*

Restaurants 🍴
Adrian Tropical Malecón
  26 *D4*

Ananda 32 *C4*
Asadero los Argentinos
  25 *D3*
Bagels 'n More 12 *C3*
Barra Payan 28 *C4*
Boga Boga 29 *C4*
Cantábrico 1 *C4*
Cappuccino Trattoria 2 *C3*
Casa del Mofongo 3 *C2*
Chino de Mariscos 21 *C3*

El Conuco 4 *C4*
Fellini 18 *C2*
Maniquí 30 *C3*
Mesón de la Cava 8 *D2*
Outback 17 *C2*
Pepperoni 6 *D2*
Samurai 16 *C2*
Sully 10 *C2*
Vesuvio del Malecón 11 *D3*
Vesuvio II 24 *C3*

Places in Santo Domingo → For listings, see pages 33-44.

Zona Colonial

The colonial city is now only about 1% of the total area of Santo Domingo but it is the first port of call for visitors, holding almost all the sights of historical interest. **Calle Las Damas**, which runs alongside the Fortress, is the oldest paved (cobbled) street in the New World and is where the wife of Diego Colón and the ladies of the court would take their evening promenade. **Plaza España** lies at the end of Calle Las Damas and has lovely views over the river. At night time there are often cultural events laid on, such as music, folk dancing or theatre, while restaurants with open-air seating add to its attractions. **Calle El Conde** runs the length of the colonial city from the entrance gate, **Puerta El Conde** in the west, via the Cathedral to the Fortaleza Ozama and the river in the east. It is a pleasant pedestrian boulevard with shops, bars and cafés.

Fortification of Santo Domingo began in 1503, with the construction of a tower to protect the entrance to the port. The city walls, only partially restored, were started in 1543 by the architect, Rodrigo de Liendo. All along the walls they built 20 defensive positions, six of them gates to the city and the others forts or bastions reserved for the military. The most important and largest fort was the **Fortaleza Ozama** ① *T809-686 0222, Mon-Sat 0930-1900, Sun 1000-1500, US$2, guides available by separate negotiation*, or Fortaleza de Santo Domingo, overlooking the river and now bounded by the Avenida Francisco Alberto Caamaño Deñó, or Avenida del Puerto, running beneath it at the water's edge. It is the oldest fortress in America, constructed 1503-1507 by Nicolás de Ovando.

Just to the west, is the **Catedral Basílica Menor de Santa María** ① *Primada de América, Isabel La Católica esquina Nouel, Mon-Sat 0900-1630, Sun for services; no shorts allowed*, the first cathedral to be founded in the New World. Its first stone was laid by Diego Colón in 1514 (although there is some dispute and some people think it was after 1520); the first architect was Alonzo Rodríguez, but there were several. It was finished in 1540 and dedicated in 1542. Little remains of the original interior decoration, because when Sir Francis Drake sacked the city in 1586 his men removed everything of value. The alleged remains of Christopher

The mystery of Columbus' bones

After his death in 1506, Columbus was buried in Valladolid, Spain. In 1509 his body was apparently removed to Sevilla, then together with that of his son Diego to Santo Domingo sometime in the 1540s. When France took control of Hispaniola in 1795, Cuba (still part of Spain) requested Columbus' remains. An urn bearing the name 'Colón' was disinterred from beneath the altar, sent to Havana and then back to the cathedral in Sevilla in 1898, when Cuba became independent. In 1877, however, during alterations and repairs in Santo Domingo cathedral, the cache of urns beneath the altar was reopened. One casket bore the inscription 'Almirante Cristóbal Colón', both outside and in. Experts confirmed that the remains were those of Columbus; the Spanish ambassador and two further experts from Spain were dismissed for concurring with the findings. A second pair of Spanish

experts denied the discovery, hence the confusion over where the admiral's bones lay. The urn that was opened in 1877 is that which is now given pride of place in the Faro a Colón.

Research in Spain in 2002-2005 cast further doubts on the bones. DNA analysis suggested that Christopher Columbus might be buried in Spain after all, or at least part of him. DNA material was extracted from three sets of bones: the one Spain claims is Christopher, the one researchers believe is his brother, Diego and a third from Christopher's son, Hernando, whose bones were never moved after his death in 1539. DNA testing on the bones held in the Faro a Colón is needed to complete the picture but permission has so far been refused. It is possible that Columbus' bones lie at either end of his exploratory journey to the Americas.

Columbus were found in 1877 during restoration work. In 1892, the Government of Spain donated the tomb in which the remains lay, a neo-Gothic wedding cake of a monument, behind the high altar, until their removal to the Faro a Colón (see below). The cathedral was fully restored for 1992, the 500th anniversary of Columbus' first voyage, with new gargoyles and sculptures at the gates showing the indigenous people when Columbus arrived. There are 14 chapels with multilingual boards explaining each one.

Parque Colón is outside the Cathedral, on its north side, next to Calle El Conde. A statue to Christopher Columbus (Cristóbal Colón) is in the middle, with a Taíno woman at his feet, a symbol now considered rather politically incorrect. The **Museo de Ambar** ① *El Conde 107 on Parque Colón, T809-221 1333, www.minube.com/rincon/museo-de-ambar-a108447, Mon-Fri 0900-1800, Sat 0900-1600, free*, is upstairs, with a shop on the ground floor selling amber, larimar, protected black coral, local gold and pearls. There is also a **Museo de Larimar** ① *Isabel la Católica 54, T809-688 1142, www.larimarmuseum.com, daily 0900-1800, free*, where you can see examples of this lovely pale blue stone found only in the Dominican Republic.

A cluster of historical buildings lies either side of Las Damas running north from the Fortaleza Ozama. The first is the **Casa de Don Rodrigo de Bastidas/Museo Infantil** ① *T809-685 5551, www.trampolin.org.do, Tue-Fri 0900-1700, Sat-Sun 1000-1800, US$2, children US$1*, built in to the city wall on Calle Las Damas in 1510. This was the house of the royal tax collector and mayor, who went on to colonize Colombia. It is built around an inner courtyard with arches around all four walls and enormous caucho trees. In 2004 it was remodelled as a children's museum, with rooms encompassing the themes

② Zona Colonial

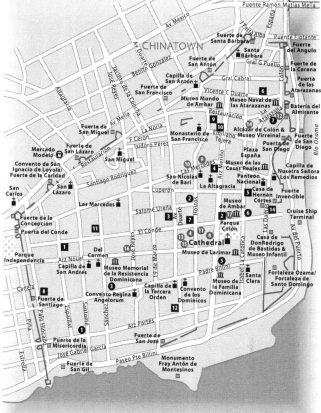

➡ Santo Domingo maps

1 Santo Domingo, page 24
2 Zona Colonial, page 27

N

200 metres
200 yards

Where to stay 🛏
Aída 1
Antiguo Hotel Europa 10
Aparthotel Condo-Parque & Venus Bar 8
Atarazana 6
Conde de Peñalba 2
Cool Hostal 9
El Beaterio 12
El Palacio 3
Francés 4
Hodelpa Caribe Colonial 5
Hostal Casa Grande 11

Hostal Nicolás de Ovando & La Résidence 14
Mercure Comercial 7

Restaurants 🍴
Anacaona 6
Angelo 7
Exquisiteses Virginia 1
Falafel 3
La Briciola 5
Mesón de Barí 2
Mesón La Quintana 6
Pat'e Palo 7

Bars & clubs 🍸
A-Club 15
Alohomora 4
Atarazana 9 12
Doubles 8
Hard Rock Café 17
Llegó 16
Maio Casa Bar 9
Mojiganga 10
Onno's 11
Parada 77 14
Proud Mary 13

The Trujillo dictatorship

In May 1930, elections were won by the armed forces commander, Rafael Leonidas Trujillo Molina, who became president. Thus began one of the most ruthless dictatorships ever seen in the Dominican Republic. With either himself or his surrogates at the helm (Héctor Trujillo, 1947-1960, and Joaquín Balaguer, 1960-1962), Trujillo embarked on the expansion of industry and public works and the liquidation of the country's debts. Nevertheless, his methods of government denied any form of representation and included murder, torture, blackmail and corruption. For 30 years he ruled supreme, dispensing favours or punishment as he deemed appropriate. During his reign, in 1937, an estimated 10,000 Haitian immigrants were rounded up and slaughtered, deepening the hatred between the two republics. The economy prospered with the expansion of the sugar industry and an influx of US capital, but much of the wealth ended up in the bank accounts of the Trujillos, as the General appropriated companies and land. Trujillo was assassinated in 1961.

of universe, family, ecology and interactive games. Beside it is the **Casa de Ovando**, the home of the man who did most to build the city. It has been restored and developed into a splendid hotel, the **Hostal Nicolás de Ovando**, see Where to stay.

The **Casa de Francia**, opposite the **Hostal Nicolás de Ovando**, was built in the early 16th century and occupied by Hernán Cortés before he went off to conquer Mexico, later housing numerous government and private occupants. Next door is the **Convento de San Ignacio de Loyola** ① *Las Damas 52 between Mercedes and El Conde, Tue-Sun 0900-1630, free*, a Jesuit monastery and church. Finished in 1743, it has been the **Panteón Nacional** since 1958. The central nave forms a cross with the lateral chapels and a bronze lamp donated by the Spanish government (General Franco) hangs in the intersection. It contains the tombs of, or memorials to, many of the country's presidents, heroes and an ornate tomb built before his death for the dictator Trujillo, the 'Benefactor of the Fatherland', but after his assassination he was not given the honour of being buried here. Cross the street again for the **Capilla de Nuestra Señora de Los Remedios**, built in the early 16th century as the private chapel of the Dávila family. By its side the Reloj de Sol (sundial) was built in 1753, near the end of Las Damas, so that court officials could tell the time.

One of the most significant historical buildings in this area is the **Museo de las Casas Reales** ① *Las Damas, T809-682 4202, daily 0900-1700, US$1*, in a reconstructed early 16th-century building which was in colonial days the Palace of the Governors and Captains-General, and of the Audiencia Real and Chancery of the Indies. The Audiencia Real was a supreme court made up of three judges, designed to check the power of the Governor, and its power extended to the rest of the Caribbean and the mainland coast around the Caribbean basin. It is an excellent colonial museum (often has special exhibits), with many items salvaged from ships sunk in local waters as well as furniture, art and military items.

Calle Las Damas opens out into the **Plaza España**, a paved open space surrounded by historical monuments with a statue of Nicolás de Ovando in the middle. It has lovely views over the river and many cafes. At night there are often cultural events, such as music, folk dancing or theatre ① *Santo Domingo de Fiesta, Fri-Sun, free*. There is a tourist information cabin with three terminals for free internet access (0900-1700). The **Alcázar de Colón** at the end of Las Damas and Emilio Tejera, is a fortified house constructed without any nails by the first Viceroy, Diego Colón, in 1510-1514 to house his court and his wife, María de Toledo. Subsequently inhabited by three generations of the Columbus family, it was the seat of the Spanish Crown in the New World until the family left for Spain in 1577 and in 1770 the building was abandoned. Now completely restored, it houses the interesting **Museo Virreinal** ① *Tue-Sat 0900-1700, Sun 0900-1600, US$1.50*, (Viceregal Museum), with religious art and colonial artefacts. **Las Atarazanas**, the Dockyards, near the Alcázar, are a cluster of 16th-century buildings which served as an arsenal, warehouses and taverns for the sailors in port, now restored to contain shops, bars and restaurants. The **Museo Naval de las Atarazanas** ① *T809-682 5834, Mon-Tue, Thu-Sat 0900-1700, Sun 0900-1300, US$0.60*, at the end, contains recovered treasure from several shipwrecks, namely the *Concepción*, *Nuestra Señora de Guadalupe* and *Conde de Tolosa*. There are accounts of the many attempts to raise numerous 17th- and 18th-century ships which sank around the island and exhibits show what life was like on board ship at that time.

Near the end of Isabel La Católica lies the only joint church and fort in Santo Domingo, the **Iglesia de Santa Bárbara**, just off Avenida Mella. Built in 1574 on the site of the city quarry, it was sacked by Drake in 1586, and destroyed by a hurricane in 1591. It was reconstructed at the beginning of the 17th century. Its design is rather lopsided and haphazard, its two towers being of completely different size and style and bearing little relation with the main entrance with its triple arches. Behind the church are the ruins of its fort, where there are good views and photo opportunities. Santa Bárbara is the patron saint of the military. The plaza in front of the church is currently in a mess awaiting renovation, having been dug up in parts for infrastructural works.

Don't miss the **Museo Mundo de Ambar** ① *Arzobispo Meriño 452, esquina Restauración, T809-682 3309, www.amberworldmuseum.com, Mon-Sat 0800-1800, Sun 0800-1300, US$1.20*, in a restored 17th-century building, which has a fascinating display of scorpions, butterflies and plants fossilized in amber, with microscopes and videos. A guided tour is recommended but not essential. The staff are informative and will teach you how to tell real from fake amber. Craftsmen also polish and shape raw amber for sale here.

Round the corner and up the hill, the **Monasterio de San Francisco** (ruins), Hostos esquina E Tejera, was the first monastery in America, constructed in the first half of the 16th century, although dates vary. Sacked by Drake and destroyed by earthquakes in 1673 and 1751, it was repeatedly repaired or rebuilt. For about 50 years until the 1930s it was used as an asylum for the insane, and there are still metal brackets in places where patients were restrained with leg chains. A hurricane closed it down for good and the ruins are now used for cultural events. Not to be missed is the free concert by Grupo Bonyé on Sunday evenings, known as Son de las Ruinas, see Entertainment, page 38.

Walk south down Hostos to the **Hospital-Iglesia de San Nicolás de Bari** (ruins), Hostos between Mercedes and Luperón, begun in 1509 by Nicolás de Ovando, completed 1552, was the first stone-built hospital in the Americas. In a cruciform plan, the three-aisled Gothic-vaulted church was used for worship while two-storey wings were used for wards to cure the sick. Also plundered by Drake, it was probably one of the best-constructed buildings of the period, it survived many earthquakes and hurricanes. In 1911 some of its walls were knocked down because they posed a hazard to passers-by; also the last of its valuable wood was taken. It is now full of pigeons.

The **Museo de la Familia Dominicana** has a collection of furniture, antiques and memorabilia from the 19th century. It is housed in the **Casa de Tostado** ① *C Padre Billini esq Arz Meriño, T809-689 5000, Mon-Sat 0900-1600, US$1*, an early 16th-century mansion with a Gothic-Isabelline double window on its northern façade. The house was the home of the writer, Francisco de Tostado, the first native professor at the university, who arrived with Nicolás Ovando's mission in 1502 and built this house in the 1530s. One block further down Padre Billini is the **Convento de los Dominicos**, built in 1510. Here in 1538 the first university in the Americas was founded.

Anyone interested in Dominican 20th-century history and resistance to the US occupations and dictatorships should visit the **Museo Memorial de la Resistencia Dominicana** ⓘ *Arzobispo Nouel 210, T809-688 4440, www.museodelaresistencia.org, Tue-Sun 0930-1800, US$4 for foreigners*, a memorial to the fighters and victims in the struggle against oppression, with permanent and temporary exhibitions, many of them educational.

East of the Río Ozama

Sans Souci, the eastern bank of the Río Ozama, is the site of a massive redevelopment project. Formerly the docks, commercial shipping was moved some years ago to Haína and a marina was constructed. More recently, a new project was initiated to develop the mouth of the Ozama and part of the Malecón to make Santo Domingo more attractive for large cruise ships. The ferry to Puerto Rico also leaves from here. The **Monumento de Caña** by the river is a reminder of the origins of the country's wealth, a huge statue of a bullock cart laden with sugar cane. Of historical importance, the Capilla de La Virgen del Rosario is on the site of the first church constructed in America, restored in 1943.

The **Faro a Colón** ⓘ *Parque Mirador del Este, T809-591 1492, Tue-Sun 0900-1700, US$1* (Columbus Lighthouse), built at great cost (and not without controversy), is an enormous concrete structure in the shape of a cross. Where the arms of the cross intersect is the mausoleum containing the supposed remains of Columbus. Spotlights can project a crucifix of light into the night sky, spectacular on a cloudy night, but very rarely lit. One of the rooms in the lighthouse is a chapel, in others, different countries have mounted exhibitions (the British exhibit concentrates on the entries for the competition to design the lighthouse: the competition was won by a British design). Slums were cleared and some of the 2000 families evicted received a paltry sum of US$50 before losing their homes. Some 100,000 people are thought to have been affected by the construction work, road building and slum clearance. In the light of the controversy the King and Queen of Spain declined an invitation to attend the 1992 celebrations and the Pope withdrew his acceptance to officially open the building. Two days before the ceremonies were to begin, President Balaguer's sister, Doña Emma, to whom he was devoted, inspected the Faro and, hours later, she died, inspiring further belief that Columbus brings bad luck and that there was a curse, or *fukú* on the building. Balaguer, who had been held responsible for the whole enterprise and who was criticized for his megalomania, also stayed away from the ceremony, while he mourned his sister. The Pope did visit shortly afterwards and said Mass on 11 October. The Pope-mobile is on show outside, waiting for the next visit, and his robes are on display inside. Photography inside permitted, but no photos in the museums, no smoking, eating, drinking or pets; guides are free, but tip; shorts above the knee not allowed.

East of the Lighthouse in the **Parque Mirador del Este** are the *cenotes* (limestone sinkholes) **Tres Ojos** ⓘ *daily, US$4, ferry to the furthest lake US$0.60, toilets, guagua* from Parque Enriquillo (Three Eyes), a popular tourist attraction. They used to be public bathing pools in the times of the Taínos, and Anacaona, the wife of Enriquillo, would bathe here. There are walkways and steps down into the caves. Although geologically interesting with beautifully clear water, vendors outside are a nuisance, while car parking attendants and guides are overpriced. Be prepared to say 'no' a lot.

West of the Río Ozama

Gazcue is a quiet, attractive residential area with expensive homes built in the 1930s and 1940s, stretching west of the Zona Colonial as far as Avenida Máximo Gómez. The **Palacio Presidencial** ① *T809-695 8000*, with a neoclassical central portico and cupola, built by Trujillo, is at the intersection of Doctor Delgado and Manuel María Castillo. It is used by the President, but guided tours of the richly decorated interior can be arranged. Opposite the Palacio's grounds are the government offices (Avenida México y 30 de Marzo). The 1955/1956 World's Fair (Feria de Confraternidad) buildings now house the Senate and Congress.

The modern city to the west is very spread out because, until recently, there was no high-rise building. Avenida George Washington (also known as the **Malecón**) runs parallel to the sea; it often becomes an open-air disco, where locals and foreigners dance the *merengue*. The annual merengue festival is held here in July. The stretch between Avenida Abraham Lincoln and Avenida Núñez de Cáceres has recently been much improved, with a wide seaside walk, piers for recreational fishing day or night which can also be used as *miradores* and there is 24-hour police presence.

The **Plaza de la Cultura**, founded by Presidente Joaquín Balaguer on Avenida Máximo Gómez, contains the country's major museums alongside the national library and the ultra-modern, white marble **National Theatre** ① *T809-687 3191*. You will have to go to the ballet or opera to see the lavish interior, although you can go to the restaurant at the back of the building for a wonderful buffet at lunchtime. The **Museo del Hombre Dominicano** ① *T809-687 3622, Tue-Sun 1000-1700, US$0.50*, traces the development of the modern Dominican, from the Amerindians, in pre-Columbian times, who were hunters and gatherers, to the Spanish conquerors and the African slaves. There were about 400,000 Taínos on the island in 1492, but only 60,000 in 1508 and they had nearly all died by 1525. Despite their rapid annihilation their influences live on in Dominican life today, all explained here. There is a large display of carnival costumes. The **Museo de Arte Moderno** ① *T809-685 2154, see Facebook, Tue-Sun 1000-1800, US$0.75*, contains a huge amount of 20th-century Dominican art on four floors. There is a permanent exhibition of national prize-winning art, with all the major artists shown by decade, as well as temporary exhibitions. The museum is particularly good as an introduction to Dominican painters and is included in most tours of Santo Domingo's many galleries. Political themes run through much of the works, particularly exploitation of children, women and Dominican society by dictators and the USA. The **Museo de Historia Natural** ① *T809-689 0106, Tue-Sun 1000-1700, US$1.25, planetarium US$0.75*, has seven main areas and halls: earth, minerals, ecology, biogeography, marine giants, birds and the Santo Domingo planetarium. Once a month, Prof Eugenio de Jesús Marcano gives a night time tour of the sky, explaining what can be seen through the telescope (reservations required and confirmation on the day, 1900, US$5). The **Museo de Historia y Geografía** ① *T809-686 6668, Tue-Sun 1000-1700, US$0.50*, has a few Taíno exhibits, but most of the displays are from the 19th and 20th centuries, starting with the Haitian invasion and following on to the American occupation. A great deal of space is taken up by artefacts belonging to Trujillo, illustrating his wealth and vanity. The museum organizes ecological excursions to different parts of the country.

Northwest of the Plaza de la Cultura is a private art collection which beautifully complements the Museo de Arte Moderno. Tucked away on the fifth floor of the Honda show room (ring the bell in the lift) is the **Museo Bellapart** ① *Av John F Kennedy esq Dr Lembert Peguero, T809-541 7721, ext 296, www.museobellapart.com, Mon-Fri 0900-1800, Sat 0900-1200, free, phone ahead for guided tours*, showcasing works of art by all the leading Dominican artists of the 20th and 21st centuries, including Jaime Colson

(1901-1975), Dionisio Pichardo (1929-2010), Clara Ledesma (1924-1999), Gaspar Mario Cruz (1929-2006) and Cándido Bidó (1936-2011). These and many other artists trace their roots and discover their identity through their technique and expression, their political and social commentary exposing injustices.

Parks

Among the attractive parks are the **Centro Olímpico**, now renamed after the world champion hurdler, **Félix Sánchez**, JF Kennedy and Máximo Gómez, in the city centre, **Parque Mirador del Este** (Autopista de las Américas, a 7-km-long *alameda*), almost entirely taken up by the sports facilities built for the PanAmerican Games, and **Parque Mirador del Sur**. The Centro Félix Sánchez is a public park, but the sporting facilities are technically only for Dominicans. The Paseo de los Indios at Parque Mirador del Sur is a 7-km-long trail, popular for walking, jogging, cycling and picnics. Avenida Anacaona runs along the north side and many desirable residences overlook the park. On Avenida José Contreras are many caves, some with lakes, in the southern cliff of Parque Mirador del Sur. Along this cliff is the Avenida Cayetano Germosén, giving access to a number of caves used at one time by Taíno Indians. The road, lined with gardens, links Avenidas Luperón and Núñez de Cáceres. **Parque Mirador del Norte** ① *T809-328 0112, www.parquemiradornorte.gob. do*, has been constructed on the banks of the Río Isabela, near Guarícano and Villa Mella. There is a boating lake, picnic areas, restaurants, jogging and cycling trails; it is known as the green lung of the city.

The **Jardín Botánico Nacional** ① *Av República de Colombia, Urbanización Los Ríos, T809-385 2611, www.jbn.gob.do, daily 0900-1800, US$5 for foreigners, US$1.25 for Dominicans, children US$1*, has a full classification of the Republic's flora. Plants endemic to the island are grown here. There are 300 types of orchid and a greenhouse for bromeliads and aquatic plants, highly recommended, especially the beautifully manicured Japanese Garden; a small trolley bus tours the extensive grounds.

Santo Domingo listings

For hotel and restaurant price codes and other relevant information, see pages 10-13.

🛏 Where to stay

Prices listed are high season rates and do not include taxes, normally 26%.

Zona Colonial *p25, map p27*
$$$$ Francés, Las Mercedes esq Arzobispo Meriño, T809-685 9331, www.accorhotels.com. A restored colonial mansion with 19 luxury rooms and lovely furnishings. The restaurant is in a beautiful courtyard and serves superb French food, expensive but recommended.
$$$$ Hostal Nicolás de Ovando, Las Damas, T809-685 9955, www.accorhotels.com. The conversion of the Casa de Ovando dating from 1502 has provided one of the most luxurious hotels in the country, a haven of cool elegance with stone walls and high, dark wooden ceilings. 104 rooms and 3 suites, spacious and comfortable, some contemporary, some colonial style, with Wi-Fi, TV, a/c, safe box. The pool overlooks the river, as do many of the rooms, small well equipped gym, massage on request, billiards and books in the lobby bar, gourmet restaurant open for all meals.
$$$ Antiguo Hotel Europa, Arzobispo Meriño esq Emiliano Tejera, T809-285 0005, www.antiguohoteleuropa.com. Built at the turn of the 20th century and lovingly restored to its former glory, complete with elegant wrought-iron balconies and fabulous tiled floors from the era. 52 rooms and suites with mahogany furniture, Wi-Fi. Meals are served in the La Terraza bar on the top floor, which has a wonderful view of the San Francisco monastery ruins and the sunset.
$$$ Atarazana, Vicente C Duarte 19, T809-688 3693, www.hotel-atarazana.com. Beautifully restored 6-room hotel right by Plaza España. Lovely rooms, cosy rather than spacious, tastefully decorated, good breakfast served in the patio where water runs down the wall, pleasant roof terrace with good views, excellent service. Zorro the cat keeps the little dogs in order.
$$$ Conde de Peñalba, El Conde esq Arzobispo Meriño facing Parque Colón, T809-688 7121, www.condepenalba.com. Great location with bar and restaurant. Rooms with TV, Wi-Fi, suites with balcony, interior rooms have no windows but are quieter than those overlooking the square.
$$$ El Beaterio, Duarte 8, T809-687 8657, www.elbeaterio.com. 16th-century guesthouse with 11 rooms set around a small courtyard with palm trees and potted plants, roof terrace and patio. Breakfast is included. A wonderful renovation with antique furniture, cast-iron beds, exquisite tiles in the bathrooms, a/c and ceiling fan, Wi-Fi. Taxi service from airport, to be booked when you make your room reservation.
$$$ El Palacio, Duarte 106 y Ureña, T809-682 4730, www.hotel-palacio.com. A colonial mansion with new extension at the rear, variety of room sizes, small swimming pool and gym, heavy wooden furniture and tiled floors, Wi-Fi. Cafeteria.
$$$ Hodelpa Caribe Colonial, Isabel La Católica 159, T809-688 7799, www.hodelpa.com. 54 rooms and suites in art deco style with a/c, TV, Wi-Fi and mini bar. A smart hotel in a good location. Bar, small restaurant, breakfast included.
$$$ Mercure Comercial, El Conde esq Hostos, T809-688 5500, www.mercure.com. 96 rooms with good bathrooms, phone, TV and fridge. Buffet breakfast and tax/service included. Good for business travellers with business centre and internet connection, Wi-Fi in communal areas.
$$ Aída, El Conde 464 y Espaillat, T809-685 7692. Very pleasant family-run accommodation. A/c rooms have no windows, rooms with fan have balcony, some rooms sleep 3. No smoking. Fairly

quiet at night, but shops below may be noisy during the day. Popular, central location, and so often full.

$$ Aparthotel Condo-Parque & Venus Bar, Palo Hincado 165, T809-333 6713, www.condo-parque.ch.vu. Dorm rooms, studios and penthouse with fan or a/c, small kitchenettes with fridges, cheap and cheerful, short or long stay available, popular meeting place, Wi-Fi, bicycle parking, restaurant/bar on first floor, snacks and breakfast, run by multilingual Walter Rüfenacht, who also runs tours to national parks including Pico Duarte and Lago Enriquillo.

$$ Cool Hostal, Hostos 357, T809-686 0120, see Facebook. Right beside ruins of San Francisco, convenient for Sun night concert, great view from The Roof bar. Small, white, minimalist rooms or suite, breakfast included, Wi-Fi in communal areas.

$ Hostel Casa Grande, Sánchez 254, T809-686 1199, see Facebook. Restored colonial house opened Dec 2012 with dorms and private rooms, communal area with pool table and darts, kitchen. Double bunk beds in dorms are new and good with plenty of head height but packed in with no space between them, lockers for backpacks, staff keen and friendly.

West of the Río Ozama *p31, map p24*
$$$$ Barceló Santo Domingo, Av Máximo Gómez esq 27 de Febrero, T809-563 5000, www.barcelo.com. One of the top hotels in the city. International style for business or leisure travellers. Lots of facilities including buffet or Japanese à la carte restaurants, casino alongside, gym, pool and spa. Good service.

$$$$ Hilton Santo Domingo, Av George Washington 500, T809-685 0000, www.hiltonsantodomingohotel.com. Modern, futuristic design, all the facilities expected of a Hilton, on the sea front, huge picture windows give fabulous views, light and airy. Outdoor pool on 7th floor, 24-hr fitness centre, business facilities.

$$$ Courtyard by Marriott, Av Máximo Gómez 50-A, Gazcue, T809-685 1010, www.marriott.com/SDQCY. Within walking distance of many places of interest. 142 very comfortable rooms and 4 suites sleeping up to 4. Free access to the internet in the lobby or in the rooms. 5 rooms are wheelchair accessible and have a connecting room for a carer. The restaurant serves breakfast, lunch and dinner, or get delivery from outside restaurants. 24-hr gym, pool, self-service laundry, safe box, fridge, coffee maker, iron and spotless bathrooms. Friendly atmosphere, no smoking.

$$ Duque de Wellington, Av Independencia 304, Gazcue, T809-682 4525, www.hotelduque.com. Conveniently located with 28 budget rooms with TV, Wi-Fi and fridge. Bar and restaurant.

$$ Foreigners Club, Canela 102, T809-689 3017, www.foreignersclubhotel.com. 10-room B&B in walking distance of the colonial zone and the Malecón, Canadian-Dominican run, helpful, easy-going but secure. Rooms of varying size and cost in art deco building, all with a/c, fan, Wi-Fi, safes, continental breakfast.

Restaurants

Zona Colonial *p25, map p27*
$$$ La Briciola, Arzobispo Merino 152, T809-688 5055, www.labriciola.com.do. Mon-Sat 1200-1500, 1800-late. Italian cuisine in courtyard of colonial house. Dine by candlelight under the brick arches or in the open air. The piano bar has live music.

$$$ La Résidence, C Las Damas, T809-685 9955. 1200-1500, 1900-2330. The restaurant is at Hostal Nicolás de Ovando and is as upmarket as the hotel, with elegant wicker furniture and beautifully presented meals served in a/c dining room or open-air courtyard. French chef, Mediterranean-style gourmet food, served to music. Very romantic.

$$$-$$ Angelo, La Atarazana 21, T809-686 3586. Open 1200-2400. Tables on Plaza España, indoors or on roof with great view over the river. Italian food with local touches, very good pizza, prawns, calamari, large portions, pleasant service.

$$$-$$ Falafel, Padre Billini esq Sánchez. T809-688 9714, see Facebook. 1200-2400. Tricky to find, but worth the effort. Mediterranean cuisine with great Lebanese and Greek food. Open-air dining or in colonial house, surrounded by paintings, relaxing atmosphere, good value and service.

$$$-$$ Mesón de Barí, Hostos 302 esq Ureña, T809-687 4091, see Facebook. 1200-0100. Great place for typical Dominican dishes from goat to crab, with rice, beans, tostones and other favourite side dishes, merengue music at weekends, unusual collection of art. The clientèle is mostly local, proving the authenticity and value of the cuisine.

$$$-$$ Pat'e Palo, La Atarazana 25, T809-687 8089. Open 1200-late. Named after the pirate, Peg Leg, who presumably liked eating and drinking after work. The first tavern in the New World was on this site, dating from 1505, although the brasserie is in a later colonial building. Meat, seafood, salads, pasta and imported cheeses and a tasting menu if you can't decide. Consistently good food. Bar serves international cocktails and several foreign beers. 1200-late. Exquisite menu, live music, excellent service and valet parking.

$$ Anacaona, El Conde 101 esq Isabel La Católica, T809-682 8253. Open 1000-2400. Excellent location and menu, outdoor seating, café/restaurant.

$$ Mesón La Quintana, La Atarazana 13, T809-687 2646. Open 1700-2400. Spanish and some Italian dishes. One of several bars and restaurants in this area.

$ Exquisiteses Virginia, Santomé 101 esq Arzobispo Portés, T809-333 9001, www.exquisitesesvirginia.com. 0700-2300. Snack bar and local restaurant, good for *quipes*, *empanadas* and *pastelitos* as well as being popular with local workers for a good set lunch with a variety of local and more international dishes.

West of the Río Ozama *p31, map p24*

$$$ Asadero los Argentinos, Av Sarasota, Plaza Jardines del Embajador, local 101, Bella Vista, T809-535 7076 and at Presidente González 5, Naco, T809-566 1499, see Facebook. 1200-2400. Excellent Argentine food with the typical *empanadas*, *chorizos* and steaks, but also the pastas much-loved by Italian-Argentines.

$$$ Boga Boga, Plaza Florida, Av Bolívar 203, Aparta Hotel Plaza Florida, T809-472 0849. Open 1100-0100. Long-running family business, Spanish, good *jamón serrano* and *chorizo*.

$$$ Cantábrico, Av Independencia 54, T809-687 5101, www.restaurantcantabrico.com.do. 1100-2400. Fresh fish and seafood, Spanish and *criollo*. Good reputation for decades.

$$$ Cappuccino Trattoria and Restaurant, Av Máximo Gómez 60, T809-689 8600. 0800-2400. Italian-owned restaurant and café in 2 sections, great Italian food, from pizza, pasta, pastries and a good coffee to more elegant dining.

$$$ El Conuco, Casimiro de Moya 152, Gazcue, T809-686 0129, see Facebook. 1100-1500, 1800-2400. Good-value buffet at lunch time and a more extensive buffet in the evening. You can also eat à la carte and try more exotic items such as *mollejitas fritas en salsa de mango* (chicken gizzards in mango sauce), *mondongo* (tripe) or *patica* (pigs' knuckles). A show of typical dancing is laid on at lunch and in the evening from 1900. Popular with tour parties.

$$$ Fellini, Roberto Pastoriza 504 esq Av Winston Churchill, T809-540 5330. Open 1900-late. Mediterranean and Italian cuisine. Fine dining. Busy bar Fri nights with music.

$$$ Maniquí, Pedro Henríquez Ureña in the Plaza de la Cultura, behind the Museo de Arte Moderno, T809-689 3030, see Facebook. From 1200. Busy at lunch time, music every night, free corkage on Mon so take your own bottle. Fine dining, very pretty food.

$$$ Mesón de la Cava, Parque Mirador del Sur, in a natural cave, T809-533 2818, www.elmesondelacava.com. 1130-1700, 1730-2400. Good steaks, live music, dancing, great experience, very popular, reserve in advance.

$$$ Mesón Iberia, Miguel Angel Monclus 165, Mirador Norte, T809-530 7200, www.mesoniberia.com.do. Tue-Sun 1130-2400. Spanish cuisine, one of the best in the country, with tapas and full menu. Great food and service.

$$$ Outback, Av Winston Churchill 25 esq Rafael Augusto Sánchez, Acrópolis Center, T809-9556 5550, www.outback.com.do. Sun-Thu 1200-2300, Fri-Sat 1200-2400. Australian franchise. Serves good steaks and salads. Free soda drink refills.

$$$ Pepperoni, Av Sarasota 23 esq Winston Churchill, Plaza Universitaria, T809-508 1330. A bit of Sushi, Thai, pasta, ribs, salads and gourmet dishes. Delicious desserts.

$$$ Samurai, Seminario 57, Ens Piantini, T809-565 1621. Mon-Sat 1200-1500, 1800-2400; Sun 1200-1600. Good Japanese and sushi bar.

$$$ Sully, Av Charles Summer 19 y Calle Caoba, Los Prados, T809-562 3389, www.restaurantsully.com. Tue-Sun 1200-1500, 1900-2400. Lots of seafood in Dominican, French and Italian styles.

$$$ Vesuvio II, Av Tiradentes 17, Naco, T809-562 6060. 1200-1500, 1800-2300. Italian more than international cuisine, better value than **Vesuvio I**. Bar, private dining room, home delivery, Italian family business for over 40 years, well thought of.

$$$ Vesuvio del Malecón, Av George Washington 521, T809-221 1954, www.restaurantvesuvio.com.do. Lunch and dinner. Established in 1954, the place to go in Santo Domingo for an expensive meal. Elegant dining overlooking the sea, Italian cuisine with seafood and pasta, as well as Caribbean specialities. Wheelchair accessible, valet parking.

$$$-$$ Adrian Tropical Malecón, Av George Washington, T809-221 1764.

(Also at Av John F Kennedy 82, Plaza Safari T809-566 8373; Av Independencia, Plaza Atala II, T809-508 0025; Av 27 de Febrero 429, esq Núñez de Cáceres, T809-472 1763; Av Abraham Lincoln 809 esq Rafael A Sánchez.) 0700-0200. Good, reliable place to try local specialities such as *mofongo*, but international dishes are also available. Perched on the waterfront on the Malecón, you can dine indoors or outdoors with the sea breeze and the waves crashing beneath you, particularly attractive at night when the rocks are lit up. Popular with local families. Service can be slow.

$$ Chino de Mariscos, Av Sarasota 38, T809-533 5249. Open 1100-late. Very good Chinese seafood, long-standing business in operation for decades.

$$-$ Ananda, Casimiro Núñez de Moya 7, Gazcue, T809-682 7153. Mon-Sat 1100-2200, Sun 1100-1500. *Cafetería* style, excellent vegetarian restaurant attached to yoga centre.

$$-$ Bagels 'n More, Fantino Falco 57, T809-540 2263. Open 0730-2200. New York bagel sandwiches, soups, salads and muffins. The only bagel place in the Dominican Republic.

$$-$ Casa del Mofongo, 27 de Febrero 299 esq Evaristo Morales, T809-541 1121. 0900-late. A long way from the centre, but famous for its *mofongo* (balls of mashed plantain and pork) and other local specialities.

$ Barra Payan, 30 de Marzo 140, T809-689 6654. Open 24 hrs. Sandwiches and tropical juices/smoothies, an all-time Dominican favourite for over 50 years and the place to come for a late-night fix. No tables, no credit cards, no parking, just counter service with a flourish, great *pan de agua*.

$ Heladería Valentino, Gustavo Mejía Ricart 114, Plaza Cataluña, or Av Bolívar 217, Plaza Juan Duahajre, T809-540 0998/809-566 0904, see Facebook. Italian-style ice cream, really creamy and lots of choice of natural flavours, also good milk shakes.

🔊 Bars and clubs

Santo Domingo *p22, maps p24 and p27*
There are **casinos** in several of the hotels,
often with nightclubs as well. The gay
nightlife scene is well covered by www.
monaga.net and most bars and clubs listed
can be found on Facebook for events and
special offers. New bars open and close
frequently in the colonial zone, check www.
colonialzone-dr.com, but it is a lively area at
night and well policed. A more local area to
try is Av Venezuela, to the east of the river,
where for 3 blocks around Av San Vicente de
Paul, you can find a stretch of bars, *colmados*
and places to eat, open air or indoors, with
a wide range of music, particularly busy
at weekends or holidays. If you want to
experience even more casual Dominican
nightlife, try a car wash, such as **Teleoferta**
on 27 de Febrero esq Máximo Gómez, now
so popular that it sometimes attracts live
bands, although mostly there is a DJ, bar,
food stalls and lots of dancing.

Bars

Atarazana 9, La Atarazana 9, Zona Colonial,
T809-688 0969. Mon-Sat 2000-late. Colonial
building, very historic, nice place, good
drinks. Live music upstairs Thu from 2200,
open bar, entry fee.

Cinema Café, Plaza de la Cultura, Av Pedro
Henriquez Ureña, T809-221 7555, www.
cinemacafe.com.do. Mon-Thu 1100-0100,
Fri 1100-0300, Sat 1600-0300, Sun 1700-
0100, Happy hour daily 1700-2000. Pleasant
café and patio with meals and tapas, while
at night there are lots of events such as live
music, poetry readings and drama. Popular
with the arts crowd.

Doubles, Arzobispo Meriño 154, T809-
688 3833, www.doublesbar.net. Colonial
building opposite the Cathedral with open
air patio as well as large indoor bar with lots
of comfy sofas, plants and a long wooden
bar, also a private lounge for parties. The
music is a mix of Latin and other styles.

Hard Rock Café, El Conde 103, T809-686
7771, www.hardrock.com. Open until
0030 Sun-Thu, 0200 Fri-Sat. Right in front
of the Cathedral and the biggest in Latin
America with a dance floor and salons for
private receptions or activities. The usual
pop memorabilia with items which once
belonged to the very famous, such as
Mick Jagger, Juan Luis Guerra, Madonna
and John Lennon.

La Parada Cervecera, Av George Washington
402 esq S Sánchez, T809-685 2072. Open
0800-2400. For a taste of car wash culture,
try this open-air bar on the Malecón, where
loud Latin music competes with traffic noise.
Popular with locals and tourists.

Maio Casa Bar, Las Mercedes 101, esq
Arzobispo Meriño, T809-682 3261, see
Facebook for events. Open Wed-Thu 2000-
0100, Fri-Sat 2000-0300, Sun 1600-2400.
Young crowd, spread out in main room,
lounge, games room or patio, live music
or electronic, local and international.

Mojiganga, Las Mercedes 154 esq Hostos,
see Facebook. 2000-late. Modern design
and decor in colonial building with central
patio, several a/c rooms and indoor and
outdoor bars. Good washrooms. Live acts
some nights.

Onno's, Hostos 157, T809-689 1183, www.
onnosbar.com. 1700-0300. An offshoot of
the ever-popular **Onno's** in Cabarete, now a
national chain, this bar-cum-restaurant has
lots of events and specials

Parada 77, Isabel La Católica 255, T809-
221 7880, see Facebook. Very busy bar
at weekends, music ranges from rock to
merengue and bachata, cover charge for
live bands, known for the writing and
artwork on the walls.

Praia, Av Gustavo Mejía Ricart 78 esq
Lope de Vega, Naco, T809-732 0230. Exotic
decoration, beautiful turquoise VIP area,
lounge and separate dining room, good
cocktails, popular place for social activities
among Dominican people, DJs play mix of
styles, house, lounge, trance.

Proud Mary, Duarte 55 esq Arzobispo Nouel, T809-689 6611. Run by María, from Spain, who serves the best sangria in the country at US$2.50, although other drinks are good too. Unusually there is no Latin music played in this 1-room bar, just classic rock, blues and jazz, with posters of the likes of the Who, the Doors and Bob Marley on the walls.

TGI Friday's, Av Winston Churchill, Plaza Acropolis, 3rd floor, T809-955 8443. 1200-late. Good food. Bar area has floor-to-ceiling windows, large crowd for happy hour.

Clubs

Alohomora, Hostos 202 esq Arzobispo Nouel, see Facebook. Fri-Sun from 2100. Gay club opened end-2012 on 2 floors. Entertainment, strippers and shows, resident DJ.

El Secreto Musical, Baltazar de los Reyes and Pimentel. Headquarters of **Club Nacional de los Soneros**, the place to come on Tue night to hear Dominican 'son'. Men in their *guayaberas* and women in high heels and smart dresses come to dance.

Ferro Café, Henríquez Ureña esq Díaz Ordóñez, Orbe Plaza, T809-540 5718, ferro_cafe@yahoo.com. Open daily until the early hours. Good music, pleasant atmosphere, good for dancing, casual and fun.

GOLD Fashion Dance Club, 27 de Febrero esq Winston Churchill at Princess Hotel & Casino, T849-201 0253, see Facebook for special nights and offers. Open after everywhere else closes, dance through to dawn and after, VIP area, good for celebrity-spotting.

Guácara Taína, Paseo de los Indios, Av Cayetano Germosén, Parque Mirador del Sur, T809-995 5853, see Facebook. 2100-0200. Spectacular setting of a huge natural cave with stalactites and indigenous pictographs. Club with all types of music, 2 dance floors. Capacity for 2000 guests. For daytime tours of the cave T809-530 2662 (0900-1700), or T809-533 1051 (1700-2100), reserve 24 hrs in advance.

Jet Set, Independencia 2253, Centro Comercial El Portal, T809-535 4145, see Facebook. www.jetsetclub.net. 2200-late, closed Sun. The place for good Latin dance music. Dress casual. Live merengue bands on a schedule basis but mostly on Mon. Livens up after midnight. Entry price depends on how famous the band is. Couples only.

Loft Lounge & Dance Club, www.loft.com.do. The website lists activities and events such as live merengue, salsa and pop. Dress casual.

Maunaloa Night Club, Centro de los Héroes 29, T809-533 2151. Open 2200-late. Live music, fashion shows and comics, dancing to Dominican music. Only open when there are scheduled activities.

Prestige Club, Máximo Gómez 60, T809-685 6276, see Facebook. DJs, special nights, dancing, lots going on, large club with capacity for 800 people, three bars, caters for a young crowd.

Rain Live Music, Plaza Progreso, Av Lope de Vega, T829-722 5118, see Facebook. Small but popular, good DJ music, a mixture of merengue, salsa, reggaeton, house, hip hop and bachata, ladies' nights and special events.

⊙ Entertainment

Santo Domingo *p22, maps p24 and p27*
Cinema
Ticket prices are around US$5. Some cinemas have discounts Mon-Wed at the earlier showing. Performance times are around 1700-2200 in most cinemas. New releases come out on Thu. English-language movies are shown in English with Spanish subtitles. There are many cinemas, of international standard and style. For a list of cinemas and what's showing, see www.supercartelera.com

Music
Son de las Ruinas, San Francisco ruins, in the colonial city, free, Sun from 1900

(sometimes earlier). The Grupo Bonyé and other invited artists play merengue, son, boleros and other Latin styles in the plaza outside the ruins, hugely popular with locals, who waste no time in getting up to dance. Stalls and shops around the edge sell snacks, beer and rum at inflated prices. Get there early for a seat or sit on the grassy slope overlooking the dance floor.

Theatres
Casa de Teatro, Arzobispo Meriño 110, T809-689 3430. Small drama workshop.
Teatro Nacional, Plaza de la Cultura, Av Máximo Gómez, T809-687 3191, for tickets. Used for drama, dance and opera, lectures and presentations.

O Shopping

Santo Domingo *p22, maps p24 and p27*
Art and crafts
Souvenirs are **leather goods, basketware, weavings** and jewellery. The ceramic **muñeca sin rostro** (faceless doll) has become a sort of symbol of the Dominican Republic. Paintings and other **art work** are on sale everywhere, but beware of the mass-produced Haitian-style naive art. Thousands of these brightly coloured, low-quality paintings are churned out for sale to tourists. Good Dominican art is for sale in the Santo Domingo galleries or you can buy direct from artists. For a list of contemporary artists and galleries, see www.art-online-rd.com. There are excellent **cigars, rum** and **coffee** at very reasonable prices.
Centro de Arte Cándido Bidó, Dr Báez 5, Gazcue, T809-685 5310, www.galeriacandidobido.com.
Colegio Dominicano de Artistas Plásticas (CODAP), El Conde 58, T809-685 6985, see Facebook. Works of local artists, prices vary. Special events held here.
Galería de Arte Nader, Calle Rafael Augusto Sánchez 22, Torre Don Roberto, Ens Piantini, T809-544 0878. The Nader family are hugely influential and stock collecters' items of Haitian, Dominican and other Latin American works of art.

The shop at the **Museo del Hombre Dominicano** sells ceramics, Taíno reproductions and works of anthropological interest.

Street sellers of Haitian or Dominican copies of Haitian naif art are not representative of what is going on in the Dominican art world and are merely gaudy paintings for tourist consumption. For details on contemporary Dominican painters, consult **Arte Contemporáneo Dominicano**, by Gary Nicolás Nader.

Cigars
10 of *Cigar Aficionado*'s 25 best cigars of 2012 were made in the Dominican Republic.
Arturo Fuente Cigar Club, Av 27 de Febrero 211, Naco, T809-683 2770, www.arturofuentecigarclub.com. One of the few places where you can buy Arturo Fuente cigars, with a walk-in humidor. Dress smartly to go in the opulent club (some rooms are decorated with real cigars), which also offers fine dining, an extensive wine cellar and whiskey collection.
Boutique del Fumador, El Conde 109, T809-685 6425, www.caobacigars.com. This is a factory outlet for Caoba cigars on the Plaza Colón. You can have a tour of the works and watch cigars being rolled.
La Leyenda del Cigarro, Las Mercedes 107 esq Hostos, T809-682 2592. Stocks premium cigars, helpful staff.

Jewellery
The native **amber** is sold throughout the country. Do not buy amber on the street, it will as likely as not be plastic. Real amber fluoresces under ultra violet light (most reputable shops have a UV light); it floats in saltwater; if rubbed it produces static electricity; except for the very best pieces it is not absolutely pure, streaks, bits of dirt, etc, are common. **Larimar**, a sea-blue stone found only in the Dominican Republic, and red and black coral are also available

Know your cigar

Cigar connoisseurs the world over argue about which country produces the best cigars; the Dominican Republic is unquestionably a contender. The area around Santiago is tobacco country. This mountain region has the ideal combination to produce quality tobacco: sunshine, good soil and cool, temperate mountain air.

In the cigar-making process the tobacco leaf comes to the drying room where it is deveined and sorted. The leaves are bunched and cured for anything up to two years. Different leaves are used for different parts of the cigar. There are three parts to a cigar: the filler, the binder and the wrapper. The filler is in the centre and is responsible for determining the strength of the cigar. It comes in three different sections: *volado*, from the base of the plant, is light in flavour; *seco* leaves are from the middle; and *ligero*, which has a full-bodied taste, is from the crown of the plant. Binder leaves, used to hold the filler, are from the same plant as the filler and go through the same ageing and curing process. These leaves are either *volado* or *seco*. The wrapper is of the highest quality and ranges from double *claro* (the lightest) to *oscuro* (the darkest). The blending of these three parts determines the overall flavour. For example, the more *volado* and fewer *ligero* leaves, the lighter the cigar will be.

Whichever cigars you have, storage is a key element to maintaining their condition. Ideally they should be kept at between 18-19°C and at 70-75% humidity.

(remember that coral is protected). Go to the shops in the amber and larimar museums (see above) for the best selection with good explanations.
Laura Tosato, Arzobispo Meriño 204, T809-685 5297, www.lauratosato.com, also in Agora Mall. Modern, pretty designs using local materials such as larimar.

Markets

Calle El Conde, now reserved for pedestrians, is the oldest shopping sector in Santo Domingo; Av Mella at Duarte is good for discount shopping. Bargaining is acceptable in markets but rarely in shops. You will not get much of a discount but it is worth a try, particularly if you are buying in bulk. There has been an explosion of shopping malls in the new city, allowing Dominicans to buy goods and fashions from the leading international chains. They also contain supermarkets, food courts and multi-screen cinemas. The newest and biggest are **Agora**, Av JF Kennedy esq Av A Lincoln, **Acrópolis**, Av Winston Churchill, **Sambil**, Av JF Kennedy esq Paseo los Aviadores, **Galería 360**, Juan Tomás Mejía esq Cotes No 32, Arroyo Hondo, **Blue Mall**, Av Winston Churchill esq Gustavo Mejía Ricart, **Megacentro**, Av San Vicente de Paúl esq Av Mella, Santo Domingo Este. **Columbus Plaza**, Arzobispo Meriño 204, Parque Colón. 3 floors of handicrafts and souvenirs.
Mercado Modelo, Av Mella esq Santomé. Open Mon-Sat 0900-1230, 1430-1700. Gift shops, handicrafts, paintings, foodstuffs; bargain to get a good price, most prices have been marked up to allow for this. Be prepared for hassling. Guides appointed to assist tourists get a 5-10% commission from the vendor.

⚬ What to do

Santo Domingo *p22, maps p24 and p27*
Art gallery tours
Santo Domingo has a large number of excellent art galleries which can be toured independently or as part of a guided tour.

The Asociación de Galerias de Arte de la República Dominicana (AGA), T809-565 3614, www.asociaciondegaleriasrd.com, is an association of some 22 galleries promoting contemporary Dominican art and offering tours of a selection of 10 influential galleries once a month on the 3rd Thu, Sep-Feb, 1900-2300.

Birdwatching
Amigos de Aves, see Facebook, organize free birdwatching walks in the Jardín Botánico, meeting at the main gate at 0700 on Sun. They have binoculars to lend participants and the 3-hr walks along paved paths are led by a member/guide. Check online for any change as occasionally they go somewhere else.
Tody Tours, José Gabriel García 105, Zona Colonial, T809-686 0882, katetody@gmail. com. Kate Wallace offers birdwatching tours all over the Dominican Republic. She has a lodge, Villa Barrancoli, in the southwest for birders, see Facebook.

Culinary tours
Tequia Experiences, Av Gustavo Mejía Ricart 69, T809-563 0019, www.tequia experiences.com. Half-day tours called Flavours of the Old City, start from La Atarazana restaurant with a multilingual guide taking you to 5 restaurants where you are served appetizers and drinks. Further afield you can do a sugar and rum tour or chocolate and clay, visiting cocoa farmers and potters.

Diving
Golden Arrow Technical Diving Center, Mustafa Kemal Ataturk 10, Local 1, Naco, Santo Domingo, T809-566 7780, www.cave diving.com.do. Technical diving courses, IANTD certification, cave and wreck diving. Denis, who speaks French, English and Spanish, is also the co-founder and President of the non-profit Fundación Espeleobuceo Hispaniola. Technical and cave diving classes are done through IANTD. Golden Arrow

divers dive all round the island, but there are a few dive sites off Santo Domingo, or at La Caleta National Park by the airport, Serious cave divers should also contact the Dominican Republic Speleological Society, www.dr-ss.com.
GUS Dive Center, Roberto Pastoriza 356, Plaza Lira II, Santo Domingo, T809-566 0818, www.gusdivecenter.com. A good dive centre in the capital with certification courses, rental gear and scheduled dive trips.

Spectator sports
Boxing Boxing matches take place frequently in Santo Domingo at the **Gimnasio-Coliseo de Boxeo** (with a capacity to seat 7000 but capable of holding 10,000 spectators) next to the baseball stadium, at the **Carlos Teo Cruz Coliseum**, at hotels and at sports clubs, where you can also see fencing, judo, karate and table tennis.
Horse racing Horse racing takes place at the **Hipódromo V Centenario** at Km 14.5 on the Autopista de las Américas, T809-687 6060, www.hvc.com, grandstand ticket US$1 (closed mid-2013 for unpaid electricity bill).
Polo Polo matches are played at weekends at Sierra Prieta, 25 mins from Santo Domingo, T809-523 8951, and at Casa de Campo, T809-523 3333, see below.

Tour operators
Chu Chu Colonial, El Conde 60 esq Isabela La Católica, T809-686 2303, www.chuchucolonial.com. A trolley bus tour decked out to look like a steam train tours the colonial city 16 times a day, 0900-1700, 45 mins, US$12 adults, US$7 children, with audio in Spanish, French, English, Italian or Russian, a fun way to orient yourself before exploring further on foot.
Colonial Tour & Travel, Arzobispo Meriño 209, T809-688 5285, www.colonialtours. com.do. A wide range of cultural and adventure tours in the city and nationwide.
Espeleogrupo Santo Domingo, Independencia 518, T809-383 4078/809-682 1577, espeleo99@yahoo.com. An

educational organization working to protect many anthropological and geological sites, to which they also arrange technical and non-technical excursions, specifically **Las Cuevas de Pomier** in San Cristóbal and the **Cuevas de las Maravillas** in La Romana.
Museo de Historia y Geografía, Santo Domingo. Organizes archaeological and historical tours in the Republic. Tours are announced in the newspapers. The co-ordinator is Vilma Benzo de Ferrer, T809-688 6952.

Other sports
Bowling Sebelén Bowling Centre (Bolera), Av Abraham Lincoln, esq Roberto Pastoriza, T809-920 0202/809-540 0101, in a large commercial plaza in Santo Domingo. Open 1000-0200. Built to host the 1997 Panamerican Bowling Games, it is said to be the world's most hi-tech bowling alley.

☉ Transport

Santo Domingo p22, maps p24 and p27
Air
Airport Aeropuerto Las Américas, 23 km east of Santo Domingo, T809-549 1253, is the main international airport for the capital, receiving flights from North and South America, Europe and the Caribbean. Aeropuerto Internacional Dr Joaquín Balaguer, at El Higuero/La Isabela is used for domestic and short-haul flights.

Immediately on arrival go to the window on your right in the arrivals hall where you buy your tourist card (if you haven't already got one) before joining the queue for immigration, otherwise you will be sent back to start all over again. There is a tourist office (helpful, will make bus reservation if you want to go straight out of Santo Domingo). BanReservas for currency exchange is in the customs hall open Sun and at night, while ATM machines are outside the customs hall in the food court area. Car hire offices are numerous as you come out of the customs hall. On departure,

the queue for check-in can be long and slow, allow plenty of time.

Leaving the airport on the ground floor, you find the expensive, individual taxis, which charge anything up to US$40 for the ride into town. If you go upstairs, outside departures, you can pick up a returning taxi for around US$25, while *colectivo* taxis cram up to 6 passengers into the vehicle and are much cheaper at about US$3. The drive from Las Américas International Airport to Santo Domingo should take no more than 30 mins (but allow 1 hr). From the capital to the airport for the return journey prices range from US$20 to US$25, depending on the company. Most large hotels have a taxi or limousine service with set fares throughout the city and to the airport. Alternatively you can get from the airport to the colonial city if you walk (long, hot, heavy traffic), or take a *motoconcho* (motorcycle taxi), to the *autopista* (main road) and then catch a *guagua* (minibus) to Parque Enriquillo. On your return, catch any bus to Boca Chica (about 10 km from the airport) or towns east and get a *motoconcho* from the junction; only really feasible if you are travelling light. If arriving late at night take a taxi. Various tour agencies also run minibuses to the airport; check with your hotel.

Bus
Local OMSA buses run along the main corridors (*corredores*), Avs 27 de Febrero, Luperón, Bolívar, Independencia, John F Kennedy, Máximo Gómez and the west of the city, US$0.30.

Long distance There is no central bus station, each company runs its own. **Metro**, 1st class (T809-227 0101 in Santo Domingo, T809-586 6062 in Puerto Plata, T809-582 9111 in Santiago, www.metroservicios turisticos.com) operate from Calle Hatuey esq Av Winston Churchill, near 27 de Febrero and have buses to **Santiago** (US$8), **Puerto Plata** (US$9) and **Sosúa**.

Caribe Tours (T809-221 4422, www.caribe tours.com.do) operates from Av 27 de Febrero esq Leopoldo Navarro, with ticket office, café, information desk, ATM, cambio and waiting area with TV; most of their services are in a/c buses, with video and toilet, punctual, good service, no smoking. They run to all parts except east of Santo Domingo, including to **La Vega** (US$5.25), **Jarabacoa** (US$7), **Santiago** (US$7), **Barahona** (US$6.75), **Dajabón** (US$8.75), **Puerto Plata** (US$8.25), **Monte Cristi** (US$8.75), **Sosúa** (US$8.25), **Sánchez** (US$8), **Samaná** (US$8) and **Río San Juan** (US$8.25). **Terrabús**, Av 27 de Febrero 445, Santo Domingo, T809-530 6926/809-531 2777, terrabus2005@yahoo.com, is an international company with services to **Haiti**, but it also has linked domestic routes to **Santiago** (T809-587 3000), **Puerto Plata** (T809-586 1977) and **Sosúa** (T809-571 1274). Their buses are comfortable, offering TV, snacks, pillows and blankets, while their terminals have food shops, toilets, TV and children's play area.

Expreso Bávaro, runs 4 times a day, US$9.50, 4 hrs, to **Punta Cana** and the east direct from Santo Domingo, T809-682 9610, to the **Friusa** bus station at Bávaro, T809-552 1678. Restrooms and snacks at **La Lechonera**, about half way. If you tell the driver which hotel you are staying at, he will stop outside or get as close as he can.

Other smaller and cheaper bus lines include **Transporte Cibao**, Caracas 112, San Carlos, after the Plaza Lama parking lot, T809-685 7210, and Av Sadhalá 4, Santiago, T809-575 5450, to **Puerto Plata**, **Sosúa** and **Santiago**; **Transporte Espinal**, Av Paris 69, T809-689 9301, www.transporteespinal.com, to **Santiago**; Astrapu buses leave from Av JF Kennedy 1, T809-221 4006, for the east: **La Romana**, **Higüey**, **Nagua**, **San Pedro de Macorís**, **Hato Mayor**, **Miches**, etc.

The easiest way to get to **Haiti** is with Terrabús (T809-472 1080, terminal at Av 27 de Febrero esq Anacaona, Plaza Criolla), Caribe Tours (T809-221 4422, terminal at Av 27 de Febrero esq Leopoldo Navarro) (both Dominican) or **Capital Coach Line** (Haitian), T809-530 8266, 27 de Febrero 455 in Santo Domingo, www.capitalcoachline. com. They all charge US$40 one way, US$75 return, child reductions, daily service. They deal with all immigration and other formalities so all you have to do is get off the bus to take care of Dominican customs. Excellent service, efficient, comfortable a/c buses, snacks and drinks provided.

There are cheaper options but they take longer and are less comfortable. A syndicate of Dominican operators runs 30-seat buses from outside the Haitian embassy, 33 Av Juan Sánchez Ramírez, just off Av Máximo Gómez between Independencia and Bolívar. 3-4 leave every morning Mon-Fri 1100-1200 and take about 7 hrs or longer to **Port-au-Prince**, depending on the amount of merchandise to be inspected by customs at the border. They return next day. Your passport must be processed in the embassy before boarding the bus. Be quick on arriving at the embassy, get through the gates, ignoring hangers on and cries of 'passport', unless you want to wait in the street and pay someone else US$10 to take your passport in. All the passports are processed together. Payments may be required. Alternatively, take a minibus to **Jimaní** from near the bridge over the Río Seco in the centre of Santo Domingo, 6-8 hrs; get a lift up to the Haitian border and then get overcharged by Haitian youths on mopeds who take you across 3 km of no-man's-land for US$3. From Haitian immigration take a lorry-bus to **Port-au-Prince**, 3-4 hrs, very dusty. You can also take Dominican public transport to **Dajabón**, cross to **Ounaminthe** and continue to **Cap Haïtien**.

Car
Car hire There are many places at the airport, on the road to the airport and on the Malecón. **Nelly** (Av Independencia 654, T809-687 7997, www.nellyracar.com, from

US$41.50 a day for a very small car with basic CDW); **Dollar** (Av Independencia 366, T809-221 7368, www.dollar.com.do, from US$47 a day); **Europcar** (Av Independencia 354, T809-688 2121, www.europcar.com.do); **Payless** (Las Américas airport, T809-549 8911, www.paylesscar.com).

Taxi
Carros públicos, or *conchos*, are shared taxis normally operating on fixed routes, 24 hrs a day, basic fare US$0.40. *Públicos* can be hired by 1 person, if they are empty, and are then called *carreras*. They can be expensive (US$3-4, more on longer routes); settle price before getting in. Fares are higher at Christmas time. *Públicos/conchos* also run on long-distance routes; ask around to find the cheapest. You can get to just about anywhere by bus or *público* from Parque Independencia, but you have to ask where to stand. *Conchos* running on a shared basis are becoming scarcer, being replaced by *carreras*.
Radio taxis charge between US$3-5 on local journeys around Santo Domingo (US$10 per hr) and are safer than street taxis, call about 20-30 mins in advance: Taxi Anacaona, T809-530 4800; Apolo Taxi, T809-537 0000; Taxi Express, T809-537 7777; Taxi Oriental, T809-549 5555; Alex Taxi, T809-540 3311; Taxi Hogar, T809-568 2825; Tecni Taxi, T809-567 2010; Maxi Taxi, T809-544 0077; Taxi Raffi, T809-687 7858.
Motorcycle taxi service, *motoconchos*, US$0.40-50, sometimes illegally take up to 3 passengers on pillion. Drivers are supposed to wear a helmet, but none of the regulations are respected. Take care.

Train
The 1st line of the new Metro (www.metro.gob.do), designed primarily to move commuters, runs from north to south of the capital beside Av Máximo Gómez to the Teatro Nacional and then west to Centro de los Héroes, while the 2nd runs west to east following Av J F Kennedy, Expreso V Centenario and Av Padre Castellanos. Line 1 (14.5 km, 16 stations) is partly overground with elevated sections in the north and partly underground, Line 2 (10.3 km, 14 stations) is underground. Services run 0600-2230 (2200 weekends) every 4-6 mins. A rechargeable subway card (*boleto viajero*) costs US$0.75 and each trip costs US$0.50, regardless of distance. You must have a *boleto viajero* to be able to buy a ticket.

🛈 Directory

Santo Domingo *p22, maps p24 and p27*
Banks Many along Isabel La Católica, see page 18. Casa de Cambio La Catedral, Sánchez, off El Conde, gives a slightly better rate than banks. **Hospitals** Clínica Abréu, Av Independencia y Beller 42, T809-688 4411, www.clinicaabreu.com.do, and adjacent Clínica Gómez Patiño, Independencia 701, T809-685 9131, are suggested for foreigners needing treatment or hospitalization. Fees are high but care is good. 24-hr emergency department. For free consultation and prescription, Padre Billini Hospital, Calle Padre Billini y Santomé, Zona Colonial, T809-333 5656, www.hospitalpadrebillini.gob.do, efficient, friendly. **Pharmacies** Farmacia San Judas Tadeo, Independencia 57 esq Bernardo Pichardo, T809-685 8165, open 24 hrs all year, home delivery.

North to Santiago

The Autopista Duarte, Autopista 1, is a four lane highway that runs northwest from Santo Domingo to Santiago de los Caballeros, with the Cordillera Central on one side and the Cordillera Septentrional on the other. From there it reduces in size and follows the length of the Cibao Valley alongside the Río Yaque del Norte to its outlet on the coast at Monte Cristi. This is the main artery through the country, used by cars, trucks, *motoconchos*, cows, horse-drawn vehicles and others.

Bonao → *For listings, see pages 51-57.*

The first town of any size just west of the Autopista Duarte is Bonao, 85 km from the centre of Santo Domingo and surrounded by rice paddies. To the east is the Falconbridge ferronickel mine, a large employer and major contributor to the region's economy. Bonao was the birthplace of the renowned artist, Cándido Bidó (1936-2011), and his legacy can be seen in the museum and art gallery which bears his name in the Plaza de la Cultura, which he founded, where you can take classes in art, music, dance and other cultural activities. There are lots of artists' workshops and galleries in and around Bonao where you can browse local talent.

There are good places to stop along the autopista for snacks and local specialities. *Parador Miguelina* has good food, sweets and juices and is reputed to have the best bathrooms of all the roadside stops on the island: good, clean, with lots of toiletries. *Típico Bonao* has an extensive menu of local delights such as guinea fowl and rabbit, offering breakfast, lunch, dinner and sandwiches in between. Their bathrooms are also good and clean. After Bonao, on the left, is the main road to Constanza.

Constanza → *For listings, see pages 51-57.*

High up in the mountains, set in a circular valley formed by a meteor, is Constanza. Dubbed the Alps of the Dominican Republic, the mountains provide a spectacular backdrop for what is a fairly ordinary town with no buildings of note. The scenery is some of the best in the country, with rivers, forests and waterfalls and there are lots of good hikes in the area. In winter, temperatures can fall to zero or lower and there may be frosts at night, but during the day it is pleasant and fresh. In the 1950s, the dictator, General Trujillo brought in 200 Japanese families to farm the land and the valley is famous for food production, potatoes, garlic, strawberries (strawberry juice is a speciality and should be tried), mushrooms and other vegetables, and for growing ornamental flowers. The main street is Calle Luperón, which runs east to west. Most of the cheap hotels and restaurants are here or nearby. La Isla gas station is at the east end, where taxis and *motoconchos* congregate. The local **tourist office** ⓘ *Juan Pablo Duarte 17, T809-539 2900*, is run by Johnny Tactuk, a fund of information, who also owns the pizzeria next door and Safari Constanza for local tours, safari.constanza@hotmail.com.

With a good, tough, 4WD you can visit the **Parque Nacional Valle Nuevo**, via the very poor but spectacular road from Constanza to San José de Ocoa, see below. The views are wonderful and you pass the geographical centre of the island, marked by four small pyramids at the Alta Bandera military post about 30 km south of Constanza. The park's alpine plateau is at an altitude of about 2640 m and has a large number of plants which are unique to the island in pine and broadleaf forests. This is a cold, wet area with temperatures ranging between -5°C and 20°C. It is the source of two major rivers, the Yuna and the Nizao. Of the 249 plant species found in the park, 97 are endemic, while of the 64 bird species there are two tanagers in the forest, the stripe-headed tanager (*Spindalis zena*) and the very pretty blue-hooded euphonia (*Euphonia musica*), which thrives on a diet of mistletoe berries. There are also thermal springs, three Amerindian cemeteries and the **Aguas Blancas** waterfall about 15 km south of town, so you can walk it if you want. The waterfall falls in three stages with a maximum drop of 87 m to a large pool at the bottom. At weekends or holidays it is very busy and lots of litter accumulates.

North of Constanza, spread across the communities of Constanza, Bonao and Jarabacoa, is the **Reserva Científica Ebano Verde**, a cloud forest reserve created to protect the tree of the same name (green ebony, *Magnolia pallescens*). So far 687 species of plants have been listed and 78 species of bird, including *el zumbadorcito* (*Mellisuga minima*), the second smallest bird in the world, found only here and in Jamaica. There is an interpretative centre at el Arroyazo, good explanations and well marked hiking trails.

La Vega to San Francisco de Macorís → *For listings, see pages 51-57.*

Further north up the Autopista Duarte is La Vega, a quiet place in the beautiful valley of La Vega Real. After the declaration of Independence on 27 February 1844, La Vega was the first place to raise the national flag, on 4 March. It was also the first town to embrace the Restoration Movement in 1863. The town is nothing special and most people only come here to change *guaguas* or buses or to visit the local archaeological sites (see below), which can be reached by hiring a taxi in the Parque Central or at the bus stations.

La Vega's **carnival** is one of the most colourful pre-Lenten festivities in the country, with elaborate masks (*caretas*) of limping devils (*diablos cojuelos*), made mostly of papier mâché. It is also the oldest carnival, having been celebrated here since 1510, when a Spanish priest organized a re-enactment of the Spanish 'Moors and Christians' tradition. Activities are held on six weekends in February and March, in the afternoons from 1500-1800. On the first Sunday there is an inaugural parade and on subsequent Saturdays and Sundays there are 'runs' by the devils. Watch out for the local custom of hitting people with *vejigas*, balls on ropes, traditionally made from cows' bladders. There is also a Children's Day, held in the Diablodromo. *Comparsas*, sponsored music groups, compete and there are competitions for the best costumes. Materials are brightly coloured and hundreds of little bells are sown into the costumes. There are currently over 60 'groups' of around 60 members, sponsored by local businesses, and thousands of people dress up every weekend. Every year they create new costumes, passing on their old ones to Bonao and other towns for their carnivals. Traditional groups include Los Broncos, Las Mazones, Las Fieras, Las Hormiguitas, Las Panteras, Los Cavernarios, Los Bestias, Los Tigres, Las Plagas, Los Pieles Rojas and Los Rocky. It is a huge, rowdy affair. There are also performances by leading merengue and bachata groups. A collection of masks can be seen in the **Casa de la Cultura** ① *Calle Independencia, Mon-Fri 0930-1200, 1400-1700, free*, which also puts on temporary art exhibitions. See also www.dominicanmasks.com.

About 5 km north, the other side of the Autopista, is the turn for **Santo Cerro**, an old convent where the image of Virgen de las Mercedes is venerated and pilgrims come every 24 September to pray to Nuestra Señora de las Mercedes. Legend has it that Columbus raised a cross on the summit of the hill in 1494. Inside the brick church on the hill is a hole in which the cross is supposed to have stood. If you continue along the road to the other side of the hill and into the valley, 6 km north of La Vega on the road to Moca, the ruins of **La Vega Vieja** ① *Mon-Sat 0900-1200, 1400-1700, US$2* (Old La Vega), can be seen. It was founded by Columbus in 1494 but destroyed by an earthquake on 2 December 1562. Bartolomé de las Casas said the first Mass here and the first baptisms of Taínos took place here, on 21 September 1496. The first protest against the treatment of Indians was also made here in 1510, by Fray Pedro de Córdoba. La Vega Vieja is now a national park and the foundations of the fortress, church and a few houses can be seen.

Conuco

At Conuco, 5 km east of Salcedo, just before Tenares on the main road towards San Francisco de Macorís, is the **Museo Hermanas Mirabal** ① *T809-577 2704, see Facebook, Tue-Sat 0930-1700, US$0.25*. The house of the Mirabal sisters, is one of the most popular museums in the country. It was built in 1954 by their mother Doña Chea, and was the second family home. The gardens are immaculately kept, with beautiful orchids in the trees and lots of other flowers and fruit. The sisters and their husbands were active in the resistance movement in the late 1950s, but Patria, Minerva and María Teresa were ambushed and murdered in 1960 on their return from visiting their husbands in prison, and are now icons for both liberty and the rights of women. The day of their assassination, 25 November, is remembered in many Latin American countries as the International Day Against Violence Towards Women. Their murder helped to lead to the downfall of General Trujillo, who was himself assassinated in May 1961. The fourth sister, Dedé, is still alive as she did not go with them that day (her house is also open to the public). The bodies of the three sisters and Minerva's husband, Manolo, are buried in the garden, which has been declared an extension of the Pantéon Nacional, where national heroes are buried.

San Francisco de Macorís

Reached from either Salcedo or the Autopista Duarte, San Francisco de Macorís lies at the foot of the Cordillera Septentrional. This is very much an agricultural city, the main crops being rice and cacao. Organic cocoa grown here is one of the country's major exports, used by chocolate manufacturers such as Green & Blacks and Godiva, and a statue at the entrance to the town is of a hand holding a cut cocoa pod. One of the major producers of cocoa beans is **Hacienda Esmeralda García Jiménez** ① *T809-547 2166, www.cacaotour.com*, which has opened to visitors and gives good, educational tours. You will learn how to germinate the beans, how to grow the trees, what fungus and pests to look out for, how to harvest the pods, all about the fermentation, drying, roasting and grinding process and finally, how to make chocolate. A small shop at the visitor's centre sells cocoa balls and chocolate.

Jarabacoa and around → *For listings, see pages 51-57.*

Jarabacoa

Jarabacoa can be reached from the Autopista Duarte on a good road which winds through some beautiful pine forests, or from the Bonao-Constanza road on a new, 26-km road through the mountains. The climate is fresh, with warm days and cool nights. It is an important agricultural area, growing coffee, flowers, strawberries, watercress and other crops. The town itself is quite modern. Everything is in walking distance and most things can be found along the main street, **Calle Mario Nelson Galán**. You can visit the coffee factory **Monte Alto** ① *Altos del Yaque, T809-574 2618, www.ramirezcoffee.com, Mon-Sat 0800-1100, 1400-1700 US$1.20 pp for groups of more than 4, US$2.50 per person for smaller groups*, where you are given an excellent guided tour explaining all the growing, drying, roasting and processing techniques done by machines and by hand. At the shop you can try and buy their coffee, including organic varieties. The local **tourist office** is on Parque Duarte and the **Cluster Ecoturístico de Jarabacoa** ① *www.jarabacoard.com*, is just beyond where the buses stop, going out of town on the right on the way to La Confluencia.

Salto Jimenoa and Salto Baiguate

The three main rivers are the **Río Jimenoa**, the **Río Baiguate** and the **Río Yaque del Sur**. The Baiguate flows into the Jimenoa and the Jimenoa then flows into the Yaque. There are several other tributaries which are being explored for new whitewater rafting locations. The Jimenoa waterfalls, **Salto Jimenoa** ① *0800-1800, US$0.50*, are worth seeing, 10 km from town with access from the new road to Constanza, although they are often crowded with tour parties. Hurricane Georges wreaked havoc in 1998, washing away the power plant and bridge by the falls. A new walkway has been made, with wobbly suspension bridges (avoid too many people on them at any one time). The falls are large, with a tremendous volume of water and consequent noise. The last wall is used for canyoning. There is another waterfall dropping 75 m over a cliff on the Río Jimenoa, which is more difficult to get to and unsigned, off the road to Constanza, so you will have to ask for directions locally or go with a group. Closer to town, off the Constanza road, are the Baiguate falls, **Salto Baiguate**, 3.5-4 km, an easy walk, there is a signpost to the falls, fourth turn on the right after **Pinar Dorado**. A path leads from the road around the hillside, hugging the side of the gorge, until you get to some steps down to a sandy river beach and the rocks beneath the falls. There are usually lots of tours to the falls by jeep or horse.

Pico Duarte

In the Cordillera Central near Jarabacoa and Constanza is Pico Duarte, at 3087 m the highest peak in the Caribbean, but only just. Its neighbour, La Pelona, is only 5 m lower at 3082 m. During the Trujillo dictatorship, when Pico Duarte was inevitably named Pico Trujillo, one of his geographers erroneously added to the height of the mountain, allegedly to impress his *jefe* (boss). To this day, most maps have Pico Duarte at 3175 m. There are several popular hiking routes, requiring differing degrees of stamina. Some of the routes take in other mountains as well. You will see a wide selection of native flora and birds, rainforest and pine forest, although much of the latter is still recovering from a fire in 2003, and pass through several different ecosystems. It is very beautiful landscape and a great experience. If you are not shrouded in cloud there is a fantastic view looking down on clouds and other mountain peaks. The most popular routes are the 46-km trail from La Ciénaga near Jarabacoa, and the 90-km trail from Mata Grande near San José

River sports

Jarabacoa is the centre for adventure sports, being blessed with three main rivers, the Río Yaque del Norte, the Jimenoa and the Baiguate, and their many tributaries. **Canyoning** is done on the Río Jimenoa amidst beautiful scenery, unless the river is too full, as you can't do it at high water. Advanced level athletes can also go canyoning at La Damajagua near Imbert. **Cascading** is done at El Salto de Jimenoa and El Salto de Baiguate, elsewhere it can be done at the Cascada Ojo de Agua near Gaspar Hernández. The Río Yaque del Norte is a Class 3 or 4 river for **rafting**. There are several short rapids in gorges with lots of rocks and boulders to negotiate, followed by calmer sections of river. The rainy season (November and May) is more exciting than the dry season because the more water there is the faster it flows. The rainy season is also the favoured time of year for **tubing**, the best rivers being the Río Yaque del Norte, the Río Jamao and the Río Isabela. **Kayaking** can be done at advanced level on the tributaries of the Río Yaque del Norte where Class 5-6 rapids are found. Beginners are taken to the lower Yaque del Norte, the Río Yasica and the lower Río Bao, which are Class 2.

de las Matas (Mata Grande – la Pelona – Pico Duarte – Tetero – Jarabacoa, five days). Whichever route you take you will have to pay a US$2.50 national park fee (passport or copy required) and hire a guide, one for every three hikers for overnight trips, US$10-20 per day, and mules, US$10 per day for baggage, US$11-12 for riding. Mules are definitely recommended for the average hiker, you can carry all your gear and water if you want, but the guide will want a mule for his gear. Guides speak only Spanish and you must pay them as well as feed them and tip them. You are not allowed to set off on your own. There are other walks in the Parque Nacional Armando Bermúdez and the adjoining Parque Nacional José del Carmen Ramírez, but they all involve some steep climbing. Guides are available at the park entrance.

La Ciénaga route At La Ciénaga the DNP has set up a nice little camp ground. You can sleep here and there is a tap in the yard for washing but facilities are very basic. The hike is moderate, for intermediate to advanced hikers, but very hard indeed for those who are not in regular training for hill climbing. Allow three days (or more if it rains, the paths turn to calf-deep mud or even flow like knee-deep rivers). Guagua from Jarabacoa to La Ciénaga US$3, or hitch (very little traffic). On your return, the last carro for Jarabacoa leaves at 1600. **Iguana Mama**, in Cabarete (see page 63) and **Rancho Baiguate** in Jarabacoa (see page 52) both offer tours of three to nine days, or a custom-designed trek is possible if they have nothing else arranged. Walking sticks/hiking poles are recommended, particularly for the journey down, which can be hard on the knees and dangerous if wet and muddy. Take adequate clothing with you; it can be cold (below 0°C) and wet; wrap your luggage in waterproof bags and take a poncho, a torch and matches. Always give way to mules or they will knock you over, even off the precipice, which is sometimes where they end up themselves.

Santiago de los Caballeros → *For listings, see pages 51-57.*

Santiago de los Caballeros is the second largest city in the Republic and chief town of the Cibao valley. The streets of the centre are busy, noisy, with lots of advertizing signs; east of the centre it becomes greener, cleaner and quieter. The Río Yaque del Norte skirts the city with Avenida Circunvalación parallel to it. There are few sites of tourist interest, this is a modern, working city, although there are some old buildings. In the colonial part look out for tiles on the walls at street corners, with the old names of the streets, put there in 1995 to mark the 500th anniversary of the founding of the city.

Arriving in Santiago

Santiago's airport receives both international and domestic flights. There are also good links by road from Santo Domingo (four-lane highway all the way) and Puerto Plata on the coast. Several bus companies have services to the city.

The long-distance bus terminals are scattered around the city and you will probably have to get a taxi to your destination. You can walk round the centre of the city but suburbs and outlying areas are best reached by bus or *carro público*. Calle del Sol is the main commercial street, with both vendors and the main shops. In the newer part of the town, Avenida Juan Pablo Duarte and Avenida 27 de Febrero have shopping plazas, banks and fast food restaurants, very much in the US style. See also Transport, page 55.

There is a **tourist office** in the basement of the Town Hall (Ayuntamiento), Avenida Juan Pablo Duarte; it has little information available, only Spanish spoken.

Places in Santiago de los Caballeros

On **Parque Duarte** are the **Catedral de Santiago Apóstol**, a neoclassical building (19th-century) containing the tombs of the tyrant Ulises Heureux and of heroes of the Restauración de la República; the **Centro de Recreo** (one of the country's most exclusive private clubs) with Moorish-style arches and the **Palacio Consistorial** (1895-1896), now the **Casa de Cultura de Santiago** ① *Calle del Sol, T809-276 5625, Mon-Sat 0800-1800,* which holds cultural and art exhibitions. Anyone interested in Santiago's carnival and folk culture should visit **Museo Folklórico Tomás (Yoryi) Morel** ① *Restauración 174, T809-582 6787,* named after the *costumbrista* painter (1906-1979) who lived and worked in Santiago. **Museo Cultural Fortaleza San Luis**, overlooking the Río Yaque del Norte, was inaugurated in 2005 as a cultural plaza and lots of artists now have their work on exhibition, alongside canon, armoured vehicles and tanks. Repair works in 2004 uncovered 18th- and 19th-century weapons and artefacts and it was decided to convert the building from an active military base to a museum. The fort, where Dominican Independence was approved in 1844, was the scene of battle in 1863 in the War of Restoration. The clock tower dates from 1885. Informal art classes became so popular that a school of art was established, **Escuela de Arte Huáscar M Rodríguez Sotomayor**, named after the philanthropist who financed much of the work on the fortress.

Other places worth visiting are the **Pontífica Universidad Católica Madre y Maestra** (founded 1962) and the **Monumento a los Héroes de la Restauración**, at the highest point in the city (panoramic views of the Cibao valley, commissioned by Trujillo in his own honour and remodelled in 1991 to include a mirador). You can climb up to the top of the monument for a panoramic view of the city, the valley and the mountains. Behind the monument is a **theatre** built by Balaguer in the 1980s, a rather impenetrable rectangular block with lots of Italian marble. This area is popular at weekends and fiestas and there are lots of bars and restaurants around the park. At carnival or any other outdoor celebration, this is the place to come. Rum shops sprout all over the open spaces and parades and parties occupy roads and squares. Along Avenida 27 de Febrero is the **León Jiménes tobacco factory**, established in 1903. The Grupo León is known worldwide for its Aurora cigars, but profits are made from the manufacturing of Marlboro cigarettes, together with its brewing industry, led by production of Presidente beer, which dominates the local market. Next to the factory is the **Centro Cultural Eduardo León Jiménes** ① *Av 27 de Febrero 146, T809-582 2315, www.centroleon.org.do, exhibitions, café and shop open Tue-Sun 1000-1900.* The state-of-the-art cultural centre opened in 2003 in celebration of the 100th anniversary of the founding of the tobacco group. There is a visual arts collection, an anthropological collection with some priceless archaeological and ethnological pieces and a bibliographical collection. There is also a replica of the first León cigar factory (the original is on Independencia), called La Aurora, with history of the family and its business.

North to Santiago listings

For hotel and restaurant price codes and other relevant information, see pages 10-13.

🛏 Where to stay

Bonao *p45*

$ Rancho Wendy, Carr Blanco 401, Los Quemados, T829-423 7072, www.rancho wendy.com. Rural backpacker's hostal in the mountains with rooms, dormitories and camp site, tents and sleeping bags for hire. Good, cheap food available. Lots of activities, hiking, mountain biking, horse riding, whitewater rafting, kayaking. *Motoconcho* from Bonao US$2.50, taxi US$6.50.

Constanza *p45*

There are several cheap and basic places to stay in town in the **$** range, usually offering TV, hot water and small but adequate rooms. Some are attached to restaurants. Make sure there is sufficient bedding to keep you warm on cold nights.

$$$-$$ Villa Pajón, Reserva Científico Valle Nuevo, T809-334 6935, www.villapajon.do. Outside Constanza before you get to the pyramids, low-impact, rustic but comfortable cabins sleep 2-9, or room in main lodge, welcoming fireplace, children's play area, lots of activities such as walking, horse riding, birdwatching or mountain biking.

$$-$ Alto Cerro, east of town, T809-539 1553, www.altocerro.com. Highly thought of, camping, 8 hotel rooms, 6 suites and 29 1-, 2- or 3-bedroom villas, strung along a rise, great view of fields in valley, zipline, excursions on horse back, bicycle and quad bike rental, very popular at weekends, cheaper during the week, Wi-Fi, grocery, restaurant serving home-grown meat, fruit and veg, playground. Shame about the caged hawks kept as pets.

$$-$ Rancho Constanza and Cabañas de la Montaña, Calle San Francisco de Macorís 99, Sector Don Bosco, east of town towards Colonia Kennedy, T809-539 3268, www. ranchoconstanza.tripod.com. Modern, rustic, Alpine-style hotel, 11 rooms or suites with kitchens, also 12 dark, basic cabins, good for families, sleep up to 5, meal plans available, home-grown fruit, cheapest rates mid-week, playground and volley ball, lovely setting, tours arranged to waterfalls and hikes up into the mountains behind the hotel.

$ Mi Casa, Sánchez 2 esq Luperón, T809-539 2764, www.hotelrestaurantmicasa.es.tl. 21 rooms of different sizes and 1-3 beds, Wi-Fi, parking, restaurant/*comedor*, great strawberry juice and strawberry jam.

$ Vista del Valle, Matilde Viñas 41, T809-292 0232, socratesgp@hotmail.com. Small but adequate rooms and good value, those on top floor have best view from outside although none has view from inside.

La Vega *p46*

Some basic hotels on Calle Cáceres, but they are not recommended; slightly better accommodation is along the highway.
$$ Rey, Restauración 3, T809-573 9797, hotelrey97@hotmail.com. Rooms with 1 or 2 beds for 2-4 people, central, good standard, clean and safe, good restaurant downstairs, friendly staff.

Jarabacoa *p48*

$$$$-$$ Gran Jimenoa, out of town on Av La Confluencia, Los Corralitos, T809-574 6304, www.granjimenoahotel.com. Large, grand hotel with huge rooms and suites in lush countryside beside the river, safe for bathing when there isn't too much water, great location, new and in good condition, comfortable, wooden furniture in natural colours, pool, jacuzzi, indoor games, room service, good restaurant with river view, local meats, packed with Dominicans at weekends.
$$$-$$ Rancho Baiguate, T809-574 4940, www.ranchobaiguate.com. Price per person, including buffet meals. Lovely countryside setting beside river, extensive gardens, 27 rooms from standard to luxury, or small, medium and large, hot water, good bathrooms. Also 2 dormitories with 9 bunk beds in each for students/groups (the hotel started out as a summer camp). Bracing unheated pool, soccer and basketball court, quad bikes, horse riding and **Maroma's Parcours**, an adventure playground for adults, butterfly house, macadamia nursery, fish farm, helpful staff and management, friendly, English spoken. Busy watersports centre with day visitors from the coast but hotel is quiet and restful.
$$ Guest-House Jarabacoa, Calle 7, Casa 8, Medina II, 10 mins walk from Parque Duarte, T809-365 9102, www.guesthouse-jarabacoa. com. Multi-lingual German owner, friendly, helpful, can arrange excursions. Rooms in pairs with bathroom, terrace and mountain view. Meals available.
$$-$ Brisas del Yaque, Luperón esq Peregrina Herrera, T809-574 4490. Small rooms but modern, with good furnishings and good bathrooms, excellent value, small balcony, TV, a/c, brick and wood decor, tiled floors, parking, good restaurant attached and close to other places to eat.
$$-$ California, on road to Constanza, Calle José Durán E 99, T809-574 6255. 25 simple rooms opening onto patio area with arches giving shade over the doors, big room sleeps 5, bathroom, hot water, fan, breakfast US$5, other meals on request, bar, small pool, popular, friendly, tours arranged to Pico Duarte, horse riding, rafting.

Santiago de los Caballeros *p50*

$$$ Aloha Sol, Calle del Sol 150, T809-583 0090, www.alohasol.com. 66 rooms and suites, very central but a bit run down so not great value, restaurant **D'Manon** with local and international food.
$$$ Hodelpa Gran Almirante Hotel and Casino, Av Estrella Sadhalá 10, Los Jardines, on road north, T809-580 1992, www. hodelpa.com. International standard rooms and suites with a/c, mini bar and 24-hr room service. Popular with business visitors, English-speaking, friendly staff, pool, fitness centre, good restaurants and tapas bar, TGI Friday's next door.
$$$-$$ Hodelpa Centro Plaza, Calle Mella 54 esq del Sol, T809-581 7000, www.hodelpa.com. Convenient location, 86 rather small rooms and suites of good standard, English spoken, very good service, fitness centre and massage parlour, restaurant overlooking the city, no parking facilities. Free shuttle from airport.
$ Colonial, Av Salvador Cucurullo 115, T809-247 3122. Small clean rooms with a/c and/or fan, good bathrooms, very hot water, fridge, TV, cheap restaurant serving good Dominican food, friendly, English spoken, luggage store, internet access, street noise but secure, the best low-budget option.

Constanza p45

All the food here is wonderfully fresh, with local ingredients such as guinea fowl and rabbit.

$ Aguas Blancas, Rufino Espinosa 54, T809-539 1561. Open 1000-until everybody goes home. Like most of Constanza, casual dining and family dining serving typical Dominican dishes. Try the *Guinea a la salsa roja*.

$ Comedor Luisa, Antonio María García 40, T809-539 2174. One of the best *comedores* in the country, meat dishes served with huge portions of rice, beans and really fresh salad, tasty and wholesome food from the area. Seating indoors or through the back in the yard, under cover.

$ Exquiteses Dilenia, Gaston F Deligne 7, T809-539 2213. Open 1000-late. Specializes in lamb, guinea fowl and rabbit dishes. For a little variety, try the mixed grill or the *cocido*. Also a hostal.

$ Lorenzo's, Luperón 83, T809-539 2008. 0800-2300. Excellent Dominican food, try the guinea fowl or rabbit cooked in wine, also sandwiches, pizza and pasta, most dishes under US$5, open for breakfast, lunch and dinner, TV.

$ Pizzería Antojitos d' Lauren, Duarte 16 beside the Red Cross, T809-539 2554. 1600-2300. Casual, plastic tables, plastic cups, chicken, sancocho, local specialities, popular at night for pizza, delicious strawberry juice.

Jarabacoa p48

Buy strawberries beside the road, locally grown, but restaurants hardly ever have them.

$$$ Aroma de la Montaña, Jamaca de Dios, T809-452 6879, www.jamacadedios. com. High up above the valley, a revolving floor gives diners a panoramic view for miles. The food is fine, the service haphazard, but the novelty value makes it worth a visit.

$$$ Rancho Restaurant, opposite Esso station. Open for lunch and dinner. Criollo and international, good food using locally grown ingredients, belongs to **Rancho**

Baiguate. The walls are lined with the work of several local artists (who often dine there with the owners).

$$$-$$ Solo Alitas Grill & Coffee, Calle Duvergé 8, T809-574 7687. Chicken wings, burgers, ribs, hot dogs and sandwiches, look out for special grill nights with all-you-can-eat barbecue food or steak nights.

$$$-$$ Vistabella Club Bar & Grill, off road to Salto Jimenoa, 5 km from town, also part of **Rancho Baiguate**. Open for lunch and dinner. Pleasant setting overlooking valley, pool, bar and excellent food, specialize in goat, guinea fowl, pigeon, duck, or for a snack ask for a plate of mixed *longaniza*, *carne salteada* and *tostones*, great with a cold beer, popular for lunch at weekends but often quiet at night.

Santiago de los Caballeros p50

There are several restaurants around the monument on Av Francia and Calle del Sol, popular on Sun.

$$$ Camp David Ranch, Ctra Luperón Km 7, the turn-off is on the right, unsigned, before the El Económico supermarket, T809-626 0578, www.campdavidranch.com. Lunch and dinner, also accommodation. A 10-min drive up a winding, paved road to the ranch. The food is good, not particularly expensive and the view is breathtaking across the Cibao Valley, especially at sunset.

$$$ El Café, Av Texas esq Calle 5, Jardines Metropolitanos, T809-587 4247. Lunch and dinner. The favourite of businessmen and the wealthy, at the upper end of the price range with white linen on the tables. Good for sea bass and rack of lamb.

$$$ Il Pasticcio, Av El Llano, esq 3, Cerros de Gurabo, T809-582 6061, www.ilpasticciord. com. Tue-Sun 1200-1530, 1900-2300. Eclectic Italian place, art work on the walls and on the plate, great for late night drinks, a time when the owner, Paolo, is frequently there for conversation.

$$$ Pedro, Calle 6 No 18, Los Jardines Metropolitanos, T809-582 2144. Spanish and other Mediterranean cuisine, modern design both in furnishings and on the plate, pleasant outdoor area, very good service, lunch or dinner.

$$$ Pez Dorado, Calle del Sol 43 (Parque Colón), T809-582 2518. Open 1200-2400. Chinese and international, good-quality but pricey food in generous portions, very popular for Sun lunch, excellent wine list.

$$$-$$ El Tablón Latino, Calle del Sol 12, T809-581 3813. View of the monument, great setting with outdoor seating for pleasant lunch, high-end Latin American fast food such as arepas and empanadas, also good steaks and salads.

$$$-$$ Kukara Macara, Av Francia 7 esq Calle del Sol, T809-241 3143, www.kukara macara.net. 1100-0200. Opposite the steps to the Monument. Rustic decor, cowboy style, lots of steak including Angus, prices up to US$20 for a huge, top-class piece of meat, also seafood, tacos, sandwiches and burgers.

$$$-$$ Noah, Calle del Sol 4, T809-971 0550. Sun-Wed 1200-2400, Thu-Sat until 0100. Restaurant and lounge, popular late night place by the Monument, live entertainment Thu, Latin American fusion food and sushi, variety of menu choices.

$$$-$$ Puerta del Sol, Calle del Sol 23 esq Daniel Espinal, T809-947 1414. 1100-2400, later Fri and Sat. Italian chef, pasta, pizza, international dishes and sandwiches, sports TV, Wi-Fi, a/c or open air dining and lounge.

$$ Olé, JP Duarte esq Independencia. 1000-0100. Restaurant serving Dominican criollo food and American-style pizzeria. Open air but under roof. Occasional live music.

🎵 Bars and clubs

Constanza *p45*
Kapioca, on the left as you go out of town at the end of the airport runway. A good bar with the best nightlife in the area.

Jarabacoa *p48*
Entre Amigos, Colón 182, T809-574 7979. Fri-Sat 2100-late. Bar and lounge above Supermercado El Cofre. Karaoke until about

2300, then loud merengue, reggaeton and other Latin styles with DJ.

Santiago de los Caballeros *p50*
Ahi Bar Dance Club, attached to **Ahi Bar Café & Grill**, R César Tolentino esq Restauración, T809-581 6779, www.ahi-bar.com. DJ music. Karaoke on Sun from 2000, big screens for music videos and sports, even in the bathrooms, Parking.
Casa Bader, Beller. Low-key bar in business since 1939, known for 'the coldest beer in the country'. They also serve excellent *quipes* to go with it.
Francifol Café, Calle del Sol 127, T809-971 5558. Popular with a young crowd and birthday parties, DJs, live music at weekends, strobe lighting and fog machines.
Lovera Bar, Estrella Sadhalá beside Central 2 Supermarket, Plaza Comercial Lovera, T809-575 5557. Lots going on, something different every night, from karaoke to traditional live music, entry depends on which DJ or band is booked. Lively with lots of dancing.
Montezuma, Av Francia esq Beller, T809-581 1111. Sun-Thu 0945-0100, Fri-Sat until 0300. Restaurant, bar and lounge with live music and vigorous dancing at weekends to merengue and bachata. On 2 floors, overlooking the Monument, open air, big screen for karaoke, Wi-Fi, parking.
Tribeca Lounge, Mauricio Alvarez 6, T809-724 5000. DJs and live bands, from hip hop to merengue, occasional special events such as foam parties or fashion shows.

🎭 Entertainment

Santiago de los Caballeros *p50*
Santiago is the home of *perico ripiao*, a folk style of merengue, which can be heard in bars and clubs alongside more modern merengue, salsa, bachata and US disco music. Things start late and go on until dawn. The monument is always a great place to hang out.

Theatre
The Gran Teatro del Cibao, T809-583 5011. Seats 15,000 in its main auditorium, sometimes shows opera, while merengue concerts and plays are put on in the smaller concert hall.

⚙ Festivals

Constanza *p45*
Jan Festival Constanza, based on agriculture and local products with a Japanese influence.
Feb Carnival, held on Sun with a parade at the end of the month, with *diablos cojuelos*, locally made costumes and masks.
Sep Fiestas Municipales are held over 4 days in the 1st week, followed by **Fundación** in the 3rd week, celebrating the founding of the town and taking in the **Día de Mercedes**.

La Vega *p46*
Feb Carnival, celebrations every Sat and Sun of the month for this, the best and most popular carnival display in the country, see page 13.

Jarabacoa *p48*
Feb Carnival, similar to that in La Vega, but on a smaller scale, rather chaotic with lots of music and rum all month.

Santiago de los Caballeros *p50*
Feb-Mar Santiago's carnival is a pagan celebration surrounding Independence and Easter. Working-class *barrios*, particularly La Joya and Los Pepines, have developed rival themes of **Los Lechones** and **Los Pepines** and there is much competition between them. The *lechones* have papier mâché masks of stylized pigs, while the *pepines* have pointed horns on their masks, often hugely decorated. The Carnival Queen is crowned the 1st Sun in Feb, with 'warm-ups' the 1st 3 Suns in Feb. Parades start the weekend before **Independence Day** (27 Feb), moving off from Las Carreras and ending up at the Monumento a los Héroes de la Restauración.

⚙ What to do

Constanza *p45*
Safari Constanza, Duarte, T809-539 2554, safari.constanza@hotmail.com. Group tours offered at weekends (or mid-week for a group of 3-4 on demand) to local sights in trucks, drinks and snacks provided. Also hiking with experienced guides in the Ebano Verde Reserve.

Jarabacoa *p48*
Whitewater rafting, canyoning, tubing, kayaking, rock climbing, horse riding, mountain biking, quad bikes, jeep safaris, paragliding and hiking are all on offer here. It is one of the starting points for climbing Pico Duarte.

Adventure sports
Rancho Baiguate (see page 52) is the biggest adventure sports centre and has a small army of Dominican and international specialist guides and instructors for each activity: river rafting, canyoning, hiking, mountain biking, horse riding.
Rancho Jarabacoa, T809-222 3202, www.ranchojarabacoa.net.
Canyoning, rafting and horse riding.

Paragliding/parapenting
Flying Tony, Jarabacoa, T809-848 3479, www.paraglidingtonydominicanrepublic. com. Training and tandem flights in the mountains and over beaches, transport and accommodation can be arranged.

⚙ Transport

Constanza *p45*
Bus
There are direct buses from **Santo Domingo**, Línea Junior, T809-539 2177, Expreso Constanza, T809-539 2134, R&R Express, T809-539 1100 and Línea Cobra, T809-539 2004, US$4.50, often via Bonao. Also buses from **Santiago**, **La Vega** and **Bonao**. From Santo Domingo you can

catch a bus on Av Independencia, just west of Parque Independencia, to **La Vega** every hour 0700-1800, get off at junction for Constanza. You can get to/from the Autopista Duarte by taking a *público* or *guagua* (US$1.50) to/from Constanza.

La Vega *p46*
Bus
Caribe Tours, T809-573 6806, Metro, T809-573 7099, and **Vegano Express**, T809-573 7079, are on Ctra La Vega, the road coming in to town from the autopista, but *guaguas* can be found on the corner of 27 de Febrero y Restauración. **Caribe Tours** has buses at least every 30 mins from Santo Domingo 0600-2000, US$5.25, returning 0645-1820.

Jarabacoa *p48*
Bus
No transport anywhere after 1800, very little after 1500. *Conchos* in town US$0.75. *Motoconcho* to **Rancho Baiguate** US$1.25. Jarabataxi, opposite Esso, beside Rancho restaurant, T809-574 4640. To **Santo Domingo**, Caribe Tours, T809-574 4796, from its own terminal off the main street, 0700, 1000, 1330, 1630 (same departure times from Santo Domingo to Jarabacoa), arrive 30 mins in advance (even earlier for the 0700 Mon bus), tickets sold only on day of departure, US$7, 2½ hrs. To **La Vega** by *guagua*, US$1.50; if you want to go to the capital or **Santiago**, they will let you off at the right place to pick up the next *guagua*. To **Constanza**, most people go back down to La Vega and up the Constanza road 10 km before Bonao. All transport can be found opposite the gas station.

Santiago de los Caballeros *p50*
Air
American Airlines fly daily from Miami with connections for New York. Jet Blue also fly from New York, as well as Boston and San Juan with connections to other US cities. Spirit flies from Fort Lauderdale.

Delta flies from New York. **Copa Airlines** flies from Panama City with connections throughout Latin America. See page 7, for domestic flights.

Bus
OMSA buses on main routes, as in Santo Domingo. All *carros públicos* have a letter indicating which route they are on; *carros* cost US$0.50, *guaguas* US$0.50. Many congregate at La Rotunda de las Pinas at the intersection of Estrella Sadalhá and Av 27 de Febrero.

Caribe Tours (Av 27 de Febrero, Las Colinas, T809-576 0790) bus to/from **Santo Domingo**, many daily, US$7; to **Puerto Plata**, US$3, every hr 0845-2145; it is easier to take **Caribe Tours** than Metro to Puerto Plata or the capital because Metro only takes passengers on standby on their Santo Domingo-Puerto Plata route. **Metro** terminal, Maimón y Duarte, T809-582 9111, a block or so towards the centre on Duarte from the roundabout at Estrella Sadhalá (opposite direction from Verizon); many buses daily Santo Domingo-Santiago. **Terrabus** has its terminal at the junction of Calle del Sol and Av Francia by the monument. Service to **Santo Domingo** with connections for the bus to **Haiti**. Other companies to and from the capital with good, a/c buses include Cibao (Caracas 112, Santo Domingo, T809-685 7120, E Sadhalá 4, Santiago, T809-575 5450) and Transporte Espinal. To **Samaná**, go to Puerto Plata and take **Caribe Tours** from there. *Guaguas* to **San José de las Matas** leave from the Puente Hermanos Patiño, by the river not far from the centre. *Guaguas* for **La Vega** go from the park at the corner of Restauración y Sabana Larga. Many other *guaguas* leave from 30 de Marzo with Salvador Cucurullo, to Puerto Plata 2 hrs, not recommended if you have lots of luggage. Cibao, Restauración almost with the corner of J P Duarte, runs buses up to **Dajabón** in the northwest near the Haitian border, 2½ hrs.

ⓘ Directory

Jarabacoa *p48*
Medical services Clínica César Terrero, at the junction, T809-574 4397.

Santiago de los Caballeros *p50*
Medical services Clínica Unión Médica, Av Juan Pablo Duarte 176, T809-226 8686, www.clinicaunionmedica.com. Hospital José María Cabral y Baez, T8095834311.

North coast

Along the north coast is a stretch of shoreline of immense beauty, with sandy beaches, cliffs, coves and mangroves sandwiched between clear, blue sea and picturesque green mountains. It is home to the historic port of Puerto Plata, fishing villages, all-inclusive resorts and guesthouses. To the west the climate is dry and the vegetation predominantly scrub and cactus, while to the east it is wetter and the vegetation lush, with the ubiquitous coconut palms towering above the beaches and greener than green golf courses.

Puerto Plata → *For listings, see pages 64-73.*

Puerto Plata, sandwiched between Mount Isabel de Torres and the sea, is the main gateway on the northern coast, but the town itself is not much visited. The old town centre comprises dilapidated wooden houses and other colonial buildings behind warehouses and the power station alongside the docks. A large renovation project is underway to restore the old world charm of the historical core, including the restoration of many Victorian houses. The seafront drive, the Malecón, sweeps along the beach for about 5 km, between the San Felipe fortress to the west on the point protecting the harbour and Long Beach to the east. Despite periodic renovations, however, Puerto Plata has little to attract overnight visitors and tourists prefer to stay in beach resorts outside town.

Arriving in Puerto Plata
Domestic and international flights use the Gregorio Luperón International Airport, 15 minutes by road from town. Taxis are for hire at the terminal, or you can walk to the main road if you have not much luggage and hail a *guagua*. **Caribe Tours**, **Metro** and many other bus companies pass through or terminate at Puerto Plata and transport links are good.

The old city and the fortress can be toured on foot as it is quite compact. For longer distances you can hop on a *motoconcho* or take a safer taxi. There are buses if you've got plenty of time and know where you are going.

Background
Puerto Plata, was founded by Nicolás de Ovando in 1502, although Columbus had sailed past the bay and named it the silver port because of the way the sun glistened on the sea. For many years it was used as a supply stop for the silver fleets on their way from Mexico to Spain, but it was prone to pirate attacks and it was eventually supplanted by Havana. Buccaneers then roamed the hills hunting wild cattle and pigs and selling the hides and meat. After the War of Restoration in the 1860s, tobacco became the supreme commodity. The profitable trade attracted merchants, many of them from Germany, and they built luxury mansions, some of which still stand. Tobacco waned at the beginning of

the 20th century, but by 1910 Puerto Plata was experiencing a boom in sugar prices and more building. Boom turned to bust with the Great Depression in the USA in the 1930s. In the 1960s investment in tourism and the construction of the **Playa Dorada** all-inclusive complex, provided thousands of jobs and is the mainstay of the region's economy.

Places in Puerto Plata
The old city is contained within Avenida Colón, the Malecón and Calle José Ramón Torres. The hub of the old town is the **Parque Central**. In the centre is an early 20th-century gazebo, or bandstand, and on the south side, the **San Felipe Cathedral** is worth a visit. Also on the Parque Central is the **Patrimonio Cultural** in a majestic building dating from 1908 where there are interesting art exhibitions. The **Museo del Ambar** ⓘ *Duarte 61 esquina Emilio Prud'home, T809-586 2848, www.ambermuseum.com, Mon-Sat 0900-1800*, (Amber Museum), houses a collection of rare amber in a renovated house built by a German tobacco merchant in 1918. The main museum is on the second floor containing amber from the Cordillera Septentrional, the mountains behind Puerto Plata, which contain the world's richest deposits of amber. Small, hot and not as good as the museum in Santo Domingo, with lots of pressure to spend money in the shop. A more interesting museum is the **Museo del Arte Taíno** ⓘ *Plaza Arawak, 2nd floor, Calle Beller, San Felipe, T809-586 7601*, which showcases Taíno art, a grave and history of the pre-Columbian people.

A visit is recommended to the **Fortaleza de San Felipe** ⓘ *US$2.50, multilingual audio guide included*, the oldest colonial fortress in the New World, on a promontory at the west end of the Malecón. Once the era of pirates and privateers was ended the fortress was long used as a prison. Juan Pablo Duarte was locked up here in 1844. The museum contains rusty armoury and photos of the excavation and renovation of the fortress, which was built in 1540. The museum is not especially interesting but if you climb the turrets you get a wonderful view of the coast and ships coming into the harbour. Outside there is a statue and monument to General Gregorio Luperón on a prancing horse. Nearby is the restored iron **lighthouse**, first lit on 9 September 1879, now surrounded by bits of fortress walls and cannon.

Around Puerto Plato
Just 1 km past Puerto Plata, a *teleférico* (cable car) runs to the summit of **Loma Isabel de Torres** ⓘ *T809-970 0501, www.telefericopuertoplata.com, daily 0830-1700, US$8.50 round trip*, an elevation of 779 m. A statue of Christ looks out over all of Puerto Plata, rather like the one in Rio de Janeiro; it also houses craft shops, a restaurant and there are beautifully manicured botanical gardens with a lovely view of the coast and mountains. Entrance is south of the Circunvalación del Sur on a paved road marked teleférico. Hiking tours up the mountain can be arranged. Hiking alone is not recommended. It is a moderate to hard hike, being quite steep in parts, and takes about three hours to get up to the top.

Just 6 km east of Puerto Plata, 4 km from the airport, is the beach resort of **Playa Dorada** with an exceptional golf course, and other sporting facilities. The Playa Dorada Resort is an umbrella name for a complex of a dozen all-inclusive hotels with over 4000 rooms, offering similar services, for example pool, tennis, golf, best booked as part of a package from abroad. Not all of them are beachfront. There is a central shopping mall, the **Playa Dorada Centro Comercial**, and lots of nightlife. The beach is a glorious sweep of golden sand around the promontory on which stand most of the hotels, while the golf course weaves in and out of the hotels not on the beach.

West of Puerto Plata → *For listings, see pages 64-73.*

Costambar

To the west of Puerto Plata and within easy striking distance of the city, is Costambar, which has a long stretch of sand with few waves, making it perfect for children. There are restaurants beside the beach and supermarkets if you want to cater for yourself. This is the best place to look for self-catering accommodation, there are lots of villas and condos, excellent value if you are in a group.

Cofresí and around

Cofresí beach has several hotels, luxury villas and apartments and is busy at weekends. **Ocean World Adventure Park** ① *www.oceanworld.net*, an enormous dolphinarium, has been built here despite opposition from conservationists and environmentalists. A huge hotel and marina come as part of the investment package. If you want to swim with dolphins it will cost you US$169-199. However, bear in mind that the dolphins have been captured against international treaties, removed from their pods (families) and fed on a diet of frozen fish and antibiotics.

One of the best natural river adventure playgrounds is the **27 Charcos**, or 27 waterfalls on the Río Damajagua ① *www.27charcos.com, daily 0800-1500, US$7 falls 1-7, US$8.50 falls 1-12, US$12.50 falls 1-27, including life jacket, helmet and guide,* 25 minutes from Puerto Plata, just after Imbert. The river cascades through rocks into deep pools, creating natural rock waterslides, dive boards and swimming pools. Several agencies offer tours as part of other excursions, but they only have time to do the first seven pools. Go independently or with Iguana Mama (see Cabarete, page 63) if you want to clamber up the full 27 and jump, dive and slide down them again. The earlier you go, the less crowded they will be, although with most of the groups at the lower seven, you won't see many people higher up anyway.

New roads and bridges have opened up beaches west of Puerto Plata, some of which are stunningly beautiful and worth visiting. Take the main road to Santiago (Highway 5) and turn right (west) at Imbert. At El Estrecho head north to the coast at **Luperón**, a typical Dominican village, with several markets selling fish, meat and vegetables, basic restaurants and baseball field. The jetty in the village is in a lagoon surrounded by mangroves and is a safe harbour for yachts and other boats. Some 3 km from the village is **Puerto Blanco Marina** ① *T809-299 4096*, surrounded by more mangroves providing a pretty setting and good protection for yachts. The marina is the place to be. The bar is popular, with a happy hour at 1700-1900 and live music some nights. The restaurant is known for its seafood and the food is cheap. Rooms are available (**$**) with a/c and hot water. Watersports include snorkelling, fishing and scuba diving. Catamaran tours are recommended as a great way to see the coast and snorkel in some lovely secluded spots where the coral is alive and healthy.

A second, full-service marina, **Marina Tropical** ① *www.marinatropical.com*, is in the process of being built. Plans include apartments and villas and a shopping complex, to be built in stages as funds permit. Mangrove areas are to be protected by the **Luperón Mangrove National Monument**.

La Isabela

① *Mon-Sat 0800-1745, US$4; there is a small museum with labels in Spanish and a brief description in English, a café, toilets and small gift shops selling artesanías. Guides are available.* Some 15 km west of Luperón is La Isabela, now a **Parque Nacional Histórico**. Here, on his second voyage, on 29 May 1493, Columbus landed with 1500 men on 17 ships. He founded the first European town in the Americas, with the first *ayuntamiento* and court, and here was said the first mass on 6 January 1494 by Fray Bernardo Boil. Only the layout of the town is visible. The story goes that Trujillo ordered the place cleaned up before an official visit, but his instructions were misunderstood and workers bulldozed the whole site, pushing the ruins into the sea. The restoration and archaeological excavation of La Isabela has uncovered a variey of ruins as well as Taíno and Macorix pottery and the first Hispanic ceramics. The Guayacán tree found growing around La Isabela was there before Columbus landed. The wood is very hard and the Guayacán is used to carve replicas of Taíno artefacts. To get there, take a tour from Puerto Plata, or a *carro público* from Villanueva y Kundhard, Puerto Plata, to La Isabela village, US$4, then a *motoconcho* to the ruins, US$8 return including wait at ruins, a lovely trip.

Alternatively, at El Estrecho, you can take the new road west to Villa Isabela and Estero Hondo. The mangrove swamp at **Caño Estero Hondo** is a reserve where manatee live. The paved road ends at **Playa La Ensenada**, a sweeping curve of beach, along which runs a sandy track lined on one side with shacks (*caseteros*) selling the catch of the day, such as lobster, crab or fish, and on the other side are tables and chairs under the trees. Fishing boats are pulled up on the sand, dogs mill about looking for scraps and the smell of wood-fired barbecues fills the air. Although busy at weekends, during the week it can be quiet and peaceful, The sand slopes gently into the water, making it safe for children, while at the northeastern end of the bay, boulders and rocks provide snorkelling opportunities. There is a hotel up on the hill behind the beach (**Hotel Ensenada**, T809-377 2233), but most people come for the day.

From here, a dirt road continues along the coast to **Punta Rusia**, another large, sandy bay with a few places to stay, rooms to rent, holiday homes, basic seafood restaurants and a dive shop. One of the more upmarket restaurants is used as a lunch stop (complete with pelican flying in looking for scraps) for boat tours to **Cayo Paraíso** (Paradise Island or Cayo Arena, T809-841 7606), a sand bar offshore surrounded by a colourful reef. There are motor boat and sailing boat trips here and to the mangroves from Puerto Plata hotels (US$75-100) and the snorkelling is excellent, but do try and discourage your guide/captain from feeding the fish, which benefits the more aggressive species and upsets the balance of nature as well as not being good for them to eat bread.

The unpaved road turns south over the hills to join the Carretera Duarte running from Santiago to Monte Cristi. Parts of the road are rough and rutted, which can be difficult after rain.

Monte Cristi

At the far northwestern tip of the Dominican Republic is Monte Cristi, a 19th-century town with a Victorian feel to it, while the sea around it is believed to hold the treasures of 179 sunken galleons. Carretera Duarte runs from Santiago to Monte Cristi, passing first through rice paddies and tobacco plantations in the valley, but about 50 km from the town the area becomes arid, with cactus and other desert plants, home to a multitude of goats. A large land and marine park stretches either side of the town along the coast, protecting the mouth of the Río Yaque del Norte, with mangroves, a lagoon and lots of channels. Its proximity to the Haitian border means that transport links are good and an airfield opened in 2006. There are several lovely old wooden houses in sore need of renovation. Just beyond the **BanReservas**, on Calle Duarte (which was the first theatre), is a large old house formerly the home of one of Trujillo's mistresses. Another, called Doña Emilia's house, is huge, with lovely fretwork and verandas. Both are due to be renovated. The town has an interesting, big old clock on the **Parque Central**, or Parque Reloj, made in France, but brought here on the train *Lavonia* on 11 March 1895. You can visit the house of **Máximo Gómez** ① *Av Mella, Mon-Sat 0800-1700*, the Dominican patriot who played an important role in the struggle for Cuban Independence and in the Dominican Restoration. Inside are pictures and mementoes of Máximo Gómez, a library with a detailed atlas of Cuba and a lot of books relating to Cuba, but very few about the Dominican Republic. The local cemetery contains several tombs of heroes of the Restoration. Between the town and Playa Juan de Bolaños there is a monument to **José Martí** (a rather lugubrious head of Martí on a stick), the Cuban poet and Independence fighter who came here in September 1892 before sailing with Máximo Gómez to liberate Cuba. The beach is nothing special and backs on to salt pans, but the coast is dominated by a large flat-topped mountain known as El Morro. Steps have been built up the hillside, making an extremely testing climb to a windy viewpoint. On 21 January, the Día de la Virgen Altagracia, thousands of people make a pilgrimage up El Morro, to pray and stay overnight. In the distance, 1 km offshore, you can see the **Cayos Siete Hermanos**. The seven cays in the Parque Nacional Monte Cristi are a sanctuary for migrating birds. Contact the **Club Nautico** ① *T809-597 2530*, for fishing or sailing trips. The beaches on the cays are the white sand of a typical desert island, although unfortunately the reef has been damaged by Haitian fishing incursions and there are not as many fish as there used to be.

East of Puerto Plata → *For listings, see pages 64-73.*

The coast east of Puerto Plata has some of the most beautiful beaches in the world, with a green backdrop of mountains descending to a narrow coastal plain, with palm trees, pale sand stretching for miles and sea of all shades of blue. Sosúa, Cabarete and Río San Juan are the main beach destinations, Cabarete being the windsurf capital of the world, having hosted many World Cup events. From all these places you can get quickly up into the mountains for hiking, cycling, horse riding or whatever you fancy away from the beach.

Sosúa

Sosúa (28 km east of Puerto Plata) is a little town with a beautiful and lively 1-km beach. Vendors' stalls and snackbars line the path along the back of the beach and you will be offered anything from sunbeds to toilets. There is a smaller public beach on the east side of town, referred to as the *playita*, or Little Beach, where you will be less bothered by vendors. The main street (correctly named Calle Pedro Clisante, but only ever referred to as Main Street, or Calle Principal in Spanish) is lined with a variety of shops, restaurants and bars. Little or no attention is paid to street names or numbers. The **El Batey** side of town (the side that houses most of the hotels and restaurants) was founded by German-Jewish refugees who settled here in 1941. A synagogue and memorial building are open to the public. The western end of the town is referred to as **Los Charamicos** (the two ends are separated by the beach); this is the older side of town, where the Dominicans themselves generally live, shop and party.

In the Puerto Plata area of the north coast, the diving is best around Sosúa. It is particularly good for first time divers, with sandy spots, reefs and interesting rock formations, while for more experienced divers there are tunnels, chimneys, overhangs and walls. Some sites are virgin, but many are fished out. In places the coral has been badly damaged and broken by overdiving. The best time of year is usually May to September, when the sea is calm and the visibility good. In high season, December to April, there can often be winds and rain which stir up the sand, reduce visibility and bring in a lot of rubbish which litters the dive sites. More conservation-minded divers should head further east to Río San Juan and the area offshore of the Laguna Grí Grí. There are varied dive sites for beginners or intermediate divers and the coral is in good condition. Lots of reef fish can be seen, and if you go over the wall you are likely to spot larger life such as barracuda.

Cabarete

Cabarete, famous for world-class windsurfing and kiteboarding, is 14 km east of Sosúa. Although it has grown considerably since French-Canadian windsurfers first staked their claim on this small fishing village it still maintains its small-town character. There is a wide range of places to stay, eat and dance the night away, with most places along the main road which runs next to the sea. The lagoon behind the main road is good for spotting water birds. The beach is long and sandy with beach bars, romantic dining spots and watersports touting for your business. Generally, the western end is for kiteboarders and the eastern end for windsurfers. Cabarete hosts international windsurfing, kiteboarding and sandcastle competitions; it also offers a variety of other adventure sports: mountain biking, horse riding, whitewater rafting and scuba diving are within easy reach. Close to town is the **Parque Nacional El Chocó**, which has caves believed to be 5 million years old and interesting routes for mountain biking and hiking.

Activities Cabarete is the place to be in June, when the town is taken over by serious windsurfers for the **Cabarete Race Week** ① *www.cabaretewindsurfing.com.* The winds are at their best for Race Week, but windsurfing takes place all year round. In summer (mid-June to mid-September) there are constant trade winds but few waves. In winter there is less wind, but the waves can be tremendous. The mornings are generally calm, but by the afternoon the bay is full of sails flitting about like butterflies on a puddle.

Kiteboarding has taken Cabarete by storm (www.cabaretekiteboarding.com). It takes place about 1 km downwind of the windsurfers at the western end of Cabarete beach on the aptly named **Kite Beach**, where there is flat water for the first 500 m and then a reef with waves. Cabarete is considered by those that know to be one of the best locations worldwide for the sport. In the summer, the sea is flat calm, with winds side-onshore, picking up around 1100-1300, making the mornings good for training. The **Kiteboarding World Cup**, has been held here several times in June, with top international kiteboarders competing. Another good spot for advanced kiteboarders, where there is smooth, flat water and afternoon winds, is La Boca, just east of town at the mouth of the Río Yasica de Sabaneta. However, it is even more popular with local families on Sundays, when the local restaurant serves up a typical seafood lunch, everyone eats, drinks, swims, catches crabs and parties. You can get there down a long, sandy track by car, taxi or motoconcho, or by boat down the river (**Islabon Jungle River Tour**, T809-667 1660, US$15).

On the outskirts of town is El Encuentro, a **surfing** beach, with a consistent 'break' off the right and left. There are several surf schools in huts along the beach catering for surfers, boogie-boarders and stand up paddle enthusiasts. Some of the surf camps offer free shuttles to Playa Encuentro early in the morning when the waves are best. Stand up paddle boarding is the newest craze in Cabarete and you will find people paddling their boards on the sea, in the lagoon and on the river.

Río San Juan

Further east along the north coast, Río San Juan is a friendly town in an area now quite a tourist attraction. For **tourist information** ① *T809-589 2831.* One major site of interest is a lagoon called **Laguna Grí Grí**. Boats take visitors through the mangrove forests into the lagoon and to see caves and rocks, notably the **Cueva de las Golondrinas**, formed by an 1846 rockslide. It is several kilometres long and filled with swallows, from which it gets its name. Expect to pay about US$30 for a boat taking one or two passengers, falling to US$6 per person on a boat trip taking more than six people. Trips to the lagoon and beach take about one hour, 0800-1800.

The main attraction here is the beach called **Playa Grande**, 5 km east of Río San Juan. Great swathes of pale sand make it one of the most beautiful beaches on the island. It is packed with people at weekends. There is public access to the beach, which is one of the longest white-sand beaches on the north coast. When the swell is up in winter this is the place to be for good surfing. On arrival at Playa Grande you will be surrounded by traders looking for your business at their restaurant or stall. Politely decline their offers of help until you have chosen a restaurant. There is construction work in this area and improvements are being made with new places to stay and renovations at the golf course. **Playa Caletón** is another gorgeous beach, smaller than Playa Grande, but very popular with Dominican families at weekends, when it can be noisy from the sound systems blaring out from their cars. During the week, however, it is quiet and you can get a delicious fish or lobster lunch served at tables on the sand under trees, but watch out for opportunistic pricing.

Playa La Preciosa was so named by surfers who come here to surf because of its beauty. It is a great place for photos and a lot more secluded than Playa Grande. *National Geographic* took one of their cover shots at this beach. It is the next left turn east after Playa Grande at the headland of the **Parque Nacional Cabo Francés Viejo**.

North coast listings

For hotel and restaurant price codes and other relevant information, see pages 10-13.

⊙ Where to stay

Puerto Plata *p58*
$$$$ Casa Colonial Beach & Spa,
Playa Dorada, T809-320 3232, www.casa colonialhotel.com. A touch of style and luxury among all the all-inclusive package hotels here. Somewhere to be pampered, inside and out, with artistic fusion food and indulgent spa treatments. 50 comfortable suites of different sizes.
$$$-$$ Tubagua Plantation Eco Village,
T809-696 6932, www.tubagua.com. Very rural, off the Ruta Panorámica from Puerto Plata to Santiago, 20 mins from airport. Rustic, timber and thatched lodges, cottages and cabins with private or shared bathrooms. Lovely views of the mountains and down to the coast, relaxed and casual atmosphere. Full breakfast included, other meals available,

good food but not cheap, or you can prepare your own. Lots of activities offered.
$$ Aparta-Hotel Lomar, Malecón 8, T809-320 8555. 18 large rooms, fridge, TV, a/c or fan, some rooms with balcony overlooking sea, small pool, good value, discounts negotiable.
$$ Villa Carolina, Virginia E Ortea 9, T829-908 2200, www.villacarolina.hostel.com. 300 m from Metro bus terminal and very central B&B, close to supermarket and restaurants. Single, double and triple rooms, use of kitchen, large common area, pool, pleasant garden, hospitable.
$$-$ SunCampDR, Calle Principal 40, Muñoz, 2.5 km inland from junction of highway by Playa Dorada, T809-320 1441, www.suncampdr.com. In Isabel Torres National Park by a river, wide variety of budget apartments, studios, cottages for short or long stays, friendly community, restaurant on site, eat in the village or prepare your own. Horse riding and other activities

including volunteering in the local batey. Run by Diana and her family, who are very helpful. 30-min walk or 10 mins by *público* to Playa Dorada or El Pueblito public beach.

$ Portofino, Hermanas Mirabal 12, T809-586 2858. About a block from the Malecón at the far eastern end of Long Beach in a residential area, 18 good-value a/c rooms, pool, playground and decent pizzeria.

Monte Cristi *p61*

$$$ Cayo Arena, Playa Juan de Bolaños, T809-579 3145. Apartments on the beach with 2 bedrooms, sleep 4, basic bathroom and kitchen, small pool, bar, security, parking.
$$$ El Morro, on the road to El Morro, outside town, T809-532 8251, www.elmorro. com.do. Delightful small hotel at the foot of the hill and across the road from the sea. Charming, comfortable rooms around a gazebo in gardens, good bathrooms, pity about the cockroaches. Bikes and kayaks available, tours can be arranged.
$$ Los Jardines, next to Cayo Arena, T809-853 0040, hotel.jardines@gmail.com. 2 bungalows each with 2 basic rooms, fan or a/c, no food or cooking facilities, quiet, parking, lovely gardens and small pool.
$ Chic Hotel Restaurant, Benito Monción 44, T809-579 2316. Town centre hotel, 50 rooms sleep 1-4, rooms at front overlook busy road, hot water, decor different in each room, good food but slow service.

Sosúa *p62*

There are several all-inclusives not listed here as well as villas and other self-catering options. Sosúa is not short of places to stay.
$$$$ Haciendas El Choco, El Choco Rd, T809-571 2932, www.elchoco.com. A good option for self-catering families or groups. Villas with swimming pool and large thatched verandas. All have telephone, maid, gardener and pool service and 24-hr electricity.
$$$$ Piergorgio Palace Hotel, Calle La Puntilla 1, T809-571 2626. Victorian-style building, facing the Atlantic Ocean for a breathtaking sunset. Perched on the cliffs, no

beach, steps lead down to the water, good snorkelling among the rocks. Elegant but faded decor, all rooms have semi-circular balcony and good bathroom. Romantic outdoor dining but food nothing special.
$$$ Casa Veintiuno, Calle Piano 1, Rpto Tavares, T809-571 4174, www.casaveintiuno. com. Modern, stylish B&B run by Belgians. Cool, white decor inside and out, 3 spacious suites with large bathrooms and every luxury. Excellent service, quiet and peaceful, in gardens with pool across the main road from the beach. Restaurant attached with open kitchen and very good food.
$$$ Sosua-by-the-Sea, Playa Chiquita, T809-571 3222, www.sosuabythesea.com. Breakfast included, meal plans available, but lots of restaurants in walking distance. Immaculate, a/c rooms and suites which sleep up to 4, pool and bar, lovely views. High seas in 2013 removed one of the beaches, but the sand will probably get washed back again soon. Good location, short walk into town.
$$ Casa Valeria, Dr Rosen 28, T809-571 3565, www.hotelcasavaleria.com. Right in the centre of town but quiet. Rooms and studios around pool, very pleasant, well equipped, good service and amenities, restaurant serves good food and you can take your own wine.
$$ Tropix, Camino Libre 7, T809-571 2291, www.tropixhotel.com. Perennially popular, 10 simple but comfortable rooms in 5 buildings around a small pool, with lush gardens in a quiet residential area, 5 mins' walk from town centre and beach. Breakfast served poolside, kitchen for guest use, fridge in room.

Cabarete *p63*

Low-rise hotels, all-inclusives, villas, condos and guesthouses line the 2-km bay. Some of them offer meal plans, but there are certainly plenty of other places to eat. There are 2 high seasons: Dec to Apr and then mid-Jun to mid-Sep, when the winds are strong and attract the windsurfing and kitesurfing crowd.

$$$$ Natura Cabañas, Perla Marina, between Sosúa and Cabarete, T809-571 1507, www.naturacabana.com. 10 thatched cabañas sleeping 2-6, hidden away in gardens by the beach, run by Chilean family. Each one is different, made from locally sourced materials, hammocks and hammock swings on the porch. Spa for steam bath, massages and beauty therapies, yoga offered beside or on the beach. Restaurants use locally caught fish, produce from kitchen garden and chef produces delectable meals for any diet on request.

$$$$-$$$ Velero Beach Resort, Calle La Punta 1, T809-571 9727, www.velerobeach. com. 4-star hotel at east end of the beach, rooms and suites can be combined to make apartments or penthouses with kitchens, all with sea view, neat lawns, pretty gardens and small pool giving view of whole bay, eating places in walking distance, excellent value out of season.

$$$$-$$$ Villa Taína, T809-571 0722, www.villataina.com. On the beach in town centre, wind/kitesurf school alongside and spa on site, rooms, studios and apartments, balcony or terrace, some rooms larger than others, comfortable, friendly service, breakfast included, restaurant on the beach, bar has good happy hour specials, comfy seating in sun or shade.

$$$$-$$ Palm Beach Condos, T809-571 0758, www.cabaretecondos.com. Spacious, deluxe condos, 2 bedroom, 2 bathroom, fully equipped kitchens, patios with ocean views, perfect for families, nannies available, studios or good value garden rooms for couples, pool, on the beach, central but quiet, no traffic noise, close to main restaurants and shops.

$$$-$$ Kitebeach, Kite Beach, T809-571 0878, www.kitebeachhotel.com Rooms from budget to superior and junior suites or apartments with balconies, best rooms in newer block, breakfast on the beach included, good value with special rates for long stays. Pool, beach bar.

$$ Alegría, between Velero and Sans Souci, T809-571 0455, www.hotel-alegria.com. Very good budget hotel with beach access, excellent service, friendly and secure, quiet yet within walking distance of all the action. Turn down by Jenny's supermarket. Rooms, studios and apartment, some with cooking facilities.

$$ Blue Moon Retreat, Los Brazos, 20 mins from Cabarete on the mountain road to Moca, T809-757 0614, www.bluemoon retreat.net. Set in 38 acres of peaceful, lush rolling farmland dotted with Royal palms and fruit trees with a stunning view of the sea, often used for yoga retreats. 4 simple bungalows with 4 suites, 1 family suite and 1 big apartment with 2 bedrooms, 2 bathrooms and kitchen, all with distinctive decor, fan, spacious living area, country breakfast, full service bar. Excellent restaurant, see page 68.

$$ Cabarete Surfcamp, T809-571 0733, www.cabaretesurfcamp.com. On the lagoon, quiet and offers every kind of accommodation, basic cottages and bungalows, to more luxurious apartments with kitchens. Prices from US$20 per person for bed, breakfast and evening meal, using facilities in washhouse. Pool, garden, terraces, shuttle to El Encuentro beach for surf lessons. Friendly crowd, good for single travellers.

$$ Extreme Hotel, T809-571 0330, see Facebook. Another dedicated kiteboarding hotel with lots of facilities for kiters and their gear and kite school. Other activities include circus school (trapeze), yoga, kickboxing, gym. Rooms with a/c and fan, full breakfast included, bar, restaurant, internet access. Skateboarding ramp.

Río San Juan *p63*

Several large all-inclusives have been built in the area, offering lots of facilities.

$$ Bahía Blanca, Gastón F Deligne 5, T809-589 2563, bahia.blanca.dr@codetel. net.do. Lovely location right on rocks above the sea, small beach either side, close to the lagoon, Playa Caletón 1 km away. 3-floor, white building, 21 rooms open out onto balcony, from where you get a great view of the coast, no pool, no TV, no a/c, restaurant open for breakfast and dinner on request. Slightly shabby and local music can be noisy at weekends, but still good value.

$$ Las Puertas del Paraíso, Carr La Payita, La Novilla, T809-729 9746, puertas.paraiso@gmail.com. Rural setting, 9 self-catering, 2-bedroom thatched bungalows around pool in a lovely garden, 2 km from beach. Very child-friendly yet romantic setting, French-run, skilful Dominican chef prepares delicious gourmet food at reasonable prices.

$$ Paraíso Beach, Playa Esmeralda, Villa Magante, T829-771 8656. Halfway between Río San Juan and Gaspar Hernández, Italian-run, 5 rustic cabins on the sand under trees, verandas, simple, quiet, peaceful. Very good Italian food using local ingredients, home-made pasta with lobster is delicious.

Restaurants

Puerto Plata *p58*

$$$ Jardín Suizo, Malecón 32, T809-586 9564. Mon-Sat 1100-2300. Lunch and dinner. Run by Swiss James and his Dominican wife, excellent Swiss food such as fondues.

$$$ La Parrillada Steak House, Av Manolo Tavarez Justo, T809-586 1401, www.laparrilladasteakhouse.com. Tue-Sun 1200-2330. On busy road with outdoor seating but not too noisy or polluted at night. Tasty *churrasco* and plenty of it. Good international menu.

$$$ Le Papillon, Villas Cofresí, T809-970 7640, www.lepapillon-puertoplata.com. German chef, Thomas, prepares hearty, tasty meals, good steaks, enormous surf 'n' turf, but also good vegan curry. Garden setting, open sided restaurant, aquariums, mosquito repellent provided in the evenings. Thomas has a turtle rescue programme, healing wounded turtles before releasing them back into the wild.

$$$-$$ Aguaceros, Malecón edif 32, near fire station, T809-587 2796. Open 1000 until

late. Steaks, seafood, burgers, Mexican, tables on sidewalk, bar.

$$$-$$ Hemingway's Café, Playa Dorada shopping mall, T809-320 2230. Open 1100-late. Predictable nautical, sport fishing theme. Good food and music, a/c, good service, fun at night and during the day, live bands at weekends, karaoke some nights.

Monte Cristi *p61*

Goat is the local speciality and you will see goats all over the roads. *Chivo picante* (spicy goat) is sold at roadside stands.

$$$-$$ El Bistro, San Fernando 26, 3 blocks from the clock, T809-579 2091. Mon-Fri 1100-1430, 1800-2400, Sat-Sun 1000-2400. Same ownership as Hotel Los Jardines, set in lovely courtyard on a corner with big wooden doors, white furniture and rocking chairs, seating in open air or under cover, seafood, lobster, goat, as well as sandwiches, salads and pasta.

$$-$ Cocomar, Calle San Fernando, by the monument to José Martí on Playa Juan Bolaños, T809-579 3354. Open 0800-2200. Good breakfast, typical Dominican dishes including *mangú*, also lunch and dinner, good fresh fish and *comida criolla*, generous portions, they will make what you want if they have the ingredients.

$$-$ Don Gaspar Restaurant & Hotel, Pte Jiménez 21 esq Rodríguez Camargo, T809-579 2477. Breakfast, lunch and dinner. Also a disco with a variety of music and requests, good breakfast menu, eggs, *mangú*, juice and coffee, Dominican and Spanish dishes.

$$-$ Lobster Shack, Playa Buen Hombre. Beachside casual restaurant but serving the freshest lobster, fish and other seafood. 20 mins' drive from highway on paved road.

$ Comedor Adela, Juan de la Cruz Alvarez 41, T809-579 2254. Lunch and dinner. Family atmosphere, lots of choice, good food, seafood or goat stew, parking available.

Sosúa *p62*

There are several restaurants on Main St serving international, French, Italian food, walk around and see what takes your fancy, they change frequently. Also several eating places along the beach, with lobster tanks, OK for lunch. Walk along and see what takes your fancy, although some can be pushy for custom. For Dominican food go to **Los Charamicos**, where there are *comedores*.

$$$ La Parrillada, at entrance to Terra Mar, just west of Los Charamicos off the highway, T809-820 5169, www.laparrillada steakhouse.com. Same ownership as in Puerto Plata, excellent steaks and seafood, huge portions, surf 'n' turf includes whole lobster, good value. Reservations can be made online.

$$$-$$ Antica Locanda, Pedro Clisante 24, T829-766 3336, see Facebook. Italian trattoria, good pasta and seafood, popular, friendly service.

$$$-$$ Orchidée, Dr Rosen 24, T829-380 0715, www.hotelorchidee.ch. Restaurant on top floor of small hotel, open sided with thatched roof, tricky stairs, lovely view, great sunset watching, breakfast and dinner, German chef, varied menu from schnitzel to Thai curry via pizza.

$$$-$ Morua Mai, Pedro Clisante 5 (Main St) by the turning to the beach, T809-571 3682, see Facebook. 0800-2300. Varied menu that includes meat, fish and sea food dishes, Dominican staples as well as pizza, pasta and burgers. Good selection of wines.

Cabarete *p63*
Wide range of places to eat and drink, lots of beach restaurants and bars with great atmosphere.

$$$ Bliss, at the entrance to Callejón de la Loma, T809-571 9721. Open 1800-late, closed Wed. Elegant setting with tables around the pool, Italian owner/chef, fusion cuisine, lots of pasta dishes, seafood and great desserts, a good place for a special night.

$$$ La Casa del Pescador, on the beach, T809-571 0760. Open 1200-2300. Excellent seafood and fish including paella. Tables on the sand if you want.

$$$ La Casita de Don Alfredo, also known as **Papi**, middle of town, beachfront. 1200-2400. Excellent seafood, large portions, don't miss *camarones a la papi*, own recipe with shrimps and spaghetti. Lobster or *langostinos* also delicious. Decorated in local style.

$$$ Miró, on the beach next to **José Oshay's**, T809-853 6848. Open 1500-2300, happy hour 1700-1900. Excellent dinners in arty atmosphere, on the expensive side. Art exhibitions held regularly. Live jazz. Sushi menu or Moroccan/Caribbean fusion.

$$$ Otra Cosa, at La Punta, around the eastern point, near **Hotel Velero**, T809-571 0897, www.lapuntacabarete.com. Delicious French-Caribbean food, romantic setting overlooking the ocean, very expensive by local standards.

$$$-$$ Blue Moon, 20 mins outside town in a village called Los Brazos on the way to Moca, T809-223 0614, www.bluemoon retreat.net. 1200-2400. Reservations essential. The only authentic East Indian restaurant in the region. Well known for feasts of up to 30 guests in thatched-roof dining area, or 90+ with buffet. Dinner served with guests on cushions on the floor with banana leaves as plates and the right hand as silverware. A typical feast features vegetable *pacoras*, tandoori or coconut chicken or fish or goat curry, spicy vegetable curries, home-made chutneys, cooling fresh salads, cinnamon-cardomom spiced rice, and a refreshing dessert.

$$$-$$ Lax, west side, on the beach, near **La Casa del Pescador**. 1100-0100. A lively place on the beach all day and night. International cuisine including a huge Mexican special and sushi. Good food and prices considering its location on the sand. Happy hour specials on drinks and snacks. Meeting place for windsurfers and kiteboarders.

$$ Casa Mami, Sabaneta de Yasica, 1 km east, next to the police station, across the road from beach. Lunch and dinner. Casual, small, thatched restaurant, Spanish-owned with authentic dishes such as garlic soup, real paella, but also Dominican specials and international dishes. Good-value daily specials for US$4.

$$ Pomodoro, on the beach, T809-571 0085, www.pomodorocabarete.com. 1100-2200. Good food at reasonable prices. Pizza a speciality. Lots of pasta. Jazz on Thu nights.

$$-$ Sandros, on the main street on the west side of town, T809-571 0723. 0830-1700. Rough and ready but nice people, good fun and great Dominican food, a 'small' portion of stew, rice, salad for US$4 is more than enough. Good for filling lunch.

$ Dick's bakery, west end of town, near La Casa Rosada grocery store, T809-571 0612. 0630-1800. Serves you the best coffee in town and fabulous breakfasts, very popular with locals.

$ Friends, next door to **Dick's**. 0700-1600. Another nice option for breakfast.

Río San Juan *p63*
$ Café de Paris, across road from Laguna Gri Grí, T809-778 0867, caylamarc@gmail.com. Colourful bar and restaurant, popular with locals and ex-pats, French-run, good food, with everything from a great burger, to Dominican fare or a fresh catch of the day. Big screens for sports TV, free Wi-Fi.

$ La Estrella, Calle Duarte 7, T809-589 2303. French-run but serving local food, a bar and restaurant doing a bit of everything, free Wi-Fi.

🎵 Bars and clubs

Puerto Plata *p58*
On Sun nights there is open-air dancing on the Malecón, with huge sound systems on the road and street vendors selling drinks. Most of the nightlife is in **Playa Dorada**, where there are clubs/discos playing a mix of merengue, salsa and international music, and casinos. The largest casino is at **Ocean World**, in Cofresí, which also puts on a glamorous Latin dance show, *Bravíssimo*. On the 4th floor of the casino building is

Lighthouse Lounge & Disco, with 360°-view, elegant, stylish, good cocktail list and good music. Wed is karaoke night.

Sosúa *p62*
Sosúa has a reputation for sex tourism, so be prepared before venturing out on a bar crawl at night. Politur is much in evidence and looking for drugs. The single male, young or old, will not be short of young, female company, There are dozens of bars and clubs in the centre, many of which changed hands and were revamped in 2012-2013. Music can be very loud, blaring out into the street, so if you want a quiet drink with conversation this might not be the place for you.

D' Latino, Main St. 2200-0400. Small dance floor and 3 bars, lots of flatscreen TVs, music is good, very popular.

Cabarete *p63*
Cabarete has quite a reputation for its nightlife. Many of the beach restaurants double as bars in the evening and are open after the sun comes up. You can dance merengue or listen to international music. Ask any local and they will point you in the direction of the party that night. Live bands play certain nights of the week.

Bambú, close to Onno's. 1100-0600. Comfortable with chairs and sofas where you can have a drink and a large place to dance until sunrise. Foam party Fri, Dominican night Sun.

José Oshay's Irish Beach Pub, beachfront, T809-571 0775. 0800-0100. Go through the José Oshay's Shopping Village, near Miró. Irish American owned, popular drinking spot, live music 5 nights a week.

Ojo Club, town centre on the beach, T829-745 8811, see Facebook. Always something going on here, live music, DJs, special nights, the best place for dancing, varied entertainment, always popular.

Onno's, town centre on the beach, T809-571 0461, www.onnosbar.com. Daily 1100-0600. Happy hour 1800-2100.

Access by Harrison's jewellers, relaxed ambience during the day but completely packed at night. DJs, Fri, Sat 2200-0300.

⊛ Festivals

Puerto Plata p58
Jun Cultural Festival, a week-long celebration of culture and the arts with dance performances and concerts held at the Fuerte de San Felipe.
Oct Merengue Festival with lots of music, dance, arts and crafts along the Malecón. Sometimes held Sep or Nov.

Monte Cristi p61
Feb Monte Cristi is famous for its pre-Lenten fiesta. On Sun the *toros* and the *civiles* compete against each other in the streets. The *toros* are people dressed in costumes with elaborate bull masks, wielding whips with a ball.

Cabarete p63
Feb Cabarete hosts an international sandcastle competition, when visitors construct fantastic mermaids, flowers, fruit and even the *Titanic*. Date flexible. **Master of the Ocean**, international triathlon with windsurfing, kitesurfing and surfing.
Jun Cabarete Race Week, windsurfing and kitesurfing activities and competitions.
Nov Dominican Republic Jazz Festival, 3 days of concerts, see Facebook.

⊙ Shopping

Puerto Plata p58
The Mercado Viejo is at Ureña and Separación and sells mostly hardware and furniture, although there is also a *botánica*, items relating to syncretist religion, witchcraft, voodoo and folk healing. The Mercado Nuevo, at Isabela de Torres and Villanueva, sells handicrafts, rum, Cuban cigars, Haitian art and other souvenirs. The Playa Dorada complex has the first real shopping mall on the north coast, called the Playa Dorada Plaza or Centro Comercial. Prices are slightly inflated, but the quality of all items, especially the locally made ceramics, jewellery and clothing, is superior to most sold by beach or street vendors. Cigars, leather goods, amber, larimar, coffee and rum can all be found here.

⊙ What to do

Puerto Plata p58
Golf
Los Mangos Golf Course, Costambar, T809-970 7750, www.losmangosgolf.com. Redesigned by PB Dye in 2010, the course has a lovely setting among fruit trees; you can snack on mangoes while you play (in season).
Playa Dorada Golf Course, T809-320 3472, www.playdoradagolf.com. Designed by Robert Trent Jones. Right in the middle of the resort. If you are staying at one of the resort hotels, green fees with caddy are discounted. The hotels offer lots of sports for their all-inclusive guests, and activities away from Playa Dorada, like horse riding, are easily arranged. Most watersports are also on offer through the hotels, but for scuba diving go to Sosúa.
Playa Grande Golf Course, Km 9, Carretera Río San Juan-Cabrera, T809-582 0860, www.playagrande.com. Wonderful ocean views with 10 holes on the water. Designed by Robert Trent Jones. Reservations essential.

Horse riding
Rancho Lorilar, Calle 3, Sabana Grande, Puerto Plata, T809-320 0498, www.lorilar ranch.com. Canadian-run ranch offering half or full-day tours catering for all levels of ability and all ages, or private riding for more experienced riders. Well run, helpful guides, trails through lovely countryside on the slopes of Mt Isabel de Torres, longer rides include swimming stop in lagoon and good food.

Monte Cristi p61
Watersports
Scuba diving is excellent in the area, with over 9 shipwrecks to explore, but there is

no organized dive operation. **Fishing** is popular. Contact the **Club Náutico**, T809-597 2530. Offshore there are barracuda, tuna, marlin, dorado and carite. If you are **sailing** in the lagoon or channels, be aware that when the tides change the water can rise or fall by about 1.5 m. There is one channel in the lagoon, which apparently has some 50 different entrances but only 1 exit.

Sosúa *p62*
Diving
There are lots of dive operations, in town and on the beach, offering tuition and boat dives. There is no jetty and no large dive boats, so you must be prepared to wade out to a small boat, with probably no shade, and be capable of getting back into the boat without a ladder after your dive, which can be tricky if it is rough.
Northern Coast Diving, Pedro Clisante 8, T809-571 1028, www.northerncoasdiving. com. Open daily 0800-1800. Long-established dive shop. Lots of courses, multilingual staff, normally taking 4-6 divers, good with novice or experienced divers, probably the most professional operation on this stretch of coast. Also excursions to Grí Grí Lagoon and Du Du Caverns and private trips to Paradise Island at Punta Rusia, all full day trips.

Cabarete *p63*
Horse riding
Rancho Montana, north coast, 1 hr east of Puerto Plata, just after Sabaneta de Yasica, T809-739 0733, www.ranchomontana.com. Riding along river beds and through mountains, a good way to see the beautiful countryside, swimming in the river, lunch, snacks, drinks, transport, full or half day tours.

Kiteboarding
Kiteclub Cabarete, T809-571 9748, www.kiteclubcabarete.com. 3-day beginner course, tuition to all levels including private VIP instruction with Jon Dodds, IKO instructor training and other courses, multilingual staff from Europe and the

Dominican Republic, also wake boarding and wake skate lessons on the river in the morning before the wind picks up.
Laurel Eastman Kiteboarding Centre, Caracol Beach Club, T809-571 0564, www.laureleastman.com. Offers good equipment and lessons at all levels charged by the hour, including women-only clinics, kite cleaning facilities, storage and sales.
Dare2Fly, next to Agualina Kite Resort, T809-571 0805, www.dare2fly.com. Good school, owned by **Vela Windsurf Centre**, offering courses for beginners and equipment rental for all levels. The centre has many facilities: a bar/restaurant, lockers, shop, parking and restrooms.

Sailing
Laser Training Center, T809-571 0640, www.caribwind.com. What started out as a windsurfing centre (Carib Bic) is now a world class laser sailing outfit, with all the latest equipment. Olympic sailors for both the 2008 and 2012 Games trained here, but beginners are also welcome.

Surfing
No Work Team, T809-866 1754, www.no workteamcabarete.com. Daily minisurf course, board rentals and surf camps. Also kitesurfing, windsurfing and stand-up paddleboarding. Wind and wave report, updated twice a week for the Cabarete area.
321 Take-Off, Playa Encuentro, T809-963 7873, www.321takeoff.com. Surfing school, run by long-time local surfer, Markus Bohm, daily surf lessons for all ages and levels. Also windsurfing and kiteboarding.

Tour operators
Iguana Mama, Main Street 74, T809-571 0908, www.iguanamama.com. Guided daily mountain biking, hiking and adventure tours as well as several multi-day tours, including Pico Duarte hike. Also contact them for whitewater rafting, canyoning and cascading.
Tours Trips Treks & Travel, T809-867 8884, www.4tdomrep.com. Organizes

customized educational, adventure and community service expeditions for small or large groups throughout the Dominican Republic, including all national parks, focusing on anthropology, history and geography. Also more traditional tours and photography safaris.

Windsurfing

The windsurfing schools are all good, with excellent equipment. They do not all stock the same, so if you have a preference it is worth contacting them in advance to see what they can supply. Board rental varies, make sure insurance is available. Schools have international staff able to offer lessons in Spanish, English, German, Russian, Italian or French. Walk along the beach and compare equipment and prices. Most of them stock other watersports equipment too, such as surf boards and kayaks.

Club Mistral, T809-571 9791, www. cabaretewindsurfing.com/mistral. Part of an international company with a team of qualified instructors. Caters for beginners to advanced and wave freaks. Instruction in English, Spanish and German. Kayaks and kiteboarding also available.

Fanatic, T809-571 0861, www.fanatic-cabarete.com. German speaking. Offers equipment rental and courses for adults. They also offer Spanish courses as well as babysitting services while you windsurf. **Café Pitu** alongside for breakfast, lunch, snacks, pizza and dinner.

Front Loop (formerly **Club Nathalie Simon**), T809-571 0848, www.cns-cabarete.com. Tuition for all levels, including children from 5 years old, who can start on the lagoon behind the beach. Also recommended for kiteboarding, surfing and stand-up paddleboarding. Multilingual staff. Bar, restaurant and infinity pool on the beach. **Vela**, T809-571 0805, www.velawindsurf. com. Reliable. Equipped with the latest in high performance gear, styled boards available for rent. Beginner courses and free windsurf clinics. Kids' club with instruction in

lots of watersports from age 6-10. Integrated with Dare2fly kiteboarding school, so you get a complete watersports service.

⊖ Transport

Puerto Plata *p58*
Air
For domestic flights, see page 7.

Gregorio Luperón International Airport (POP) on the north coast receives scheduled and charter flights from North America (Miami, New York, Montréal, Toronto) and from Europe (Amsterdam, Dusseldorf, Frankfurt, London). Airlines include **American Airlines**, United, jetBlue, **Air Canada**, WestJet, Condor and Thompson Flights.

There are many charter flights from various airports in the UK, mostly booked by package tour companies, but spare seats are sold on a flight-only basis, see www.charterflights.co.uk/flights/dominican_republic/puerto_plata/.

From the Caribbean TCI Sky King from Providenciales. **American Eagle** from San Juan. Some flights are seasonal.

Airport Gregorio Luperón International Airport (POP), T809-586 0219/586 0408, serves the entire north coast. It is 15-20 mins from Puerto Plata, 7 mins from Sosúa and 20 mins from Cabarete. Taxi from airport to Puerto Plata or Cabarete US$35, to Sosúa US$25, plus tip, for up to 4 people. Guaguas and carros públicos run along the main road and will pick up drop you off at the entrance to the airport for US$1 to Sosúa, motoconchos (from the car park) cost about US$5. Small bank for exchange (closed weekends), car hire agencies and a few shops. Tipping for baggage handlers (in overalls) is about US$2 per bag and they will expect something just for picking up a bag.

Bus and taxi
Local *Motoconchos*, US$0.60 almost anywhere in town, negotiate a fare for longer distances. *Guaguas*, leave Parque Central, more frequently, from the hospital

on Circunvalación Sur to destinations along the north coast. Taxis can be found around the Parque Central or on Circunvalación Sur near **Caribe Tours**. Check the fare before you get in.

Long distance Metro (T809-586 6063, Beller y 16 de Agosto), and **Caribe Tours** (T809-586 4544, at Caribe Centro Plaza, Camino Real, just off the Circunvalación Sur), run a/c coaches to/from Santo Domingo, 4 hrs, US$9. To Santiago, every hour on the hour, 1000-1800, US$3. To La Vega US$4. Alternatively you can use the *guagua* system, changing at each town, but this will take much longer, be more uncomfortable and more costly as each leg of the journey will cost you about US$1.

Car
Rental is best arranged at the airport, more choice than in town. **Avis**, airport, T809-586 0496. **Honda**, Carrera Luperón 2.5 km, T809-586 3136, at the airport, T809-586 0233. **Puerto Plata Rent a Car**, Beller 7, Puerto Plata, T809-586 3141. **Nelly Rent a Car**, Playa Dorada, T809-320 4888, at the airport, T809-586 0505.

Monte Cristi *p61*
Bus and taxi
Taxis and *motoconchos* collect at the corner of Mella and Duarte. For long distance, **Caribe Tours** is on Rodríguez Camargo esq Mella, services to **Dajabón** (34 km, border town opposite Ounaminthe in Haiti, 6 buses daily from Santo Domingo via Monte Cristi) and **Santiago**.

Sosúa *p62*
Bus and taxi
In Sosúa, transport congregates by the Texaco station and the junction of Calle Dr Rosen and the Ctra. *Motoconcho* (motorcycle taxi), US$0.40 (US$0.50 at night) to anywhere in town. A taxi to/from Puerto Plata costs US$25, a *guagua* US$0.60 and a

carro público US$1, or US$7 if you take the whole car. **Caribe Tours** (T809-571 3808) from **Santo Domingo**, US$8.

Car and motorcycle
Rentals are everywhere, shop around for prices. **Asociación de Renta Moto Sosúa Cabarete**, rents by the hour or the day, depending on type.

Cabarete *p63*
Bus and taxi
Cabarete-Sosúa US$10, airport US$35, Puerto Plata US$40. Always check price with driver before setting off. *Guagua* to Sosúa US$0.60. *Motoconcho* US$0.60 anywhere in town, negotiate price for anywhere further, price doubles at night.

Cycle
Rental from **Iguana Mama** (see Tour operators, above) on the main street at the east end of town next to **Fanatic Windsurf School**, rents well-maintained mountain bikes by the day or week. All have front suspension. They include helmets, water bottles, repair kit and spare tubes and bike insurance with all bike rentals. A variety of tours also available. More sedate bikes available from **Dutch Bicycle Rental Cabarete**, next to Onno's Bar, T829-284 6700, see Facebook. Prices from US$5.

Río San Juan *p63*
Bus and taxi
Guagua from Sosúa, 1¼ hrs, may have to change in Gáspar Hernández. Transport stops at the junction of Duarte and the main road.

❶ Directory

Puerto Plata *p58*
Immigration Dirección General de Migración, 12 de Julio 33, T809-586 2364.
Medical services Hospital Ricardo Limardo, J E Kunhardt, T809-586 2210/586 2237. There are several doctors with clinics.

Samaná Peninsula

The Samaná Peninsula is in the far northeast of the country, geologically the oldest part of the island, a finger of land which used to be a separate island. In the 19th century the bay started to silt up to such an extent that the two parts became stuck together and the resulting land is now used to grow rice. Previously the narrow channel between the two was used as a handy escape route by pirates evading larger ships. A ridge of hills runs along the peninsula, green with fields and forests. There are several beautiful beaches, which have not been overdeveloped or 'improved', fringed with palm trees and interspersed with looming cliffs. They have become popular with Europeans, many of whom were so attracted by the laid-back lifestyle they set up home here, running small hotels and restaurants. Whale watching is a big attraction, January to March, when the humpbacks come to the Bahía de Samaná to breed. This is one of the best places in the world to get close to the whales and a well-organized network of boats takes out visitors to see them.

Arriving in Samaná

Getting there

A new toll road has been built from Santo Domingo to the international airport, Prof Juan Bosch, at El Catey, on the northern coast of the Samaná Peninsula, which has cut driving times from the capital from 4½ hours to around two hours. The Autopista del Nordeste is an interesting drive, passing through an African palm plantation (the stumps of dead trees look awful, but young palms are growing between them), cattle pastures surrounding by flowering 'living fences', then the start of the Cordillera Oriental, part of the national park of Los Haitises, where the hills look like upside down egg cartons, followed by rice fields where herons stalk. Another new toll road runs from the airport along the northern coast of the peninsula to Las Terrenas, from where a non-toll road continues to Samaná. Known as the Boulevard Turístico del Atlántico, the road twists and turns as it climbs the hill, giving spectacular views down to the coast. After driving through the red cliffs where the road has been carved out of the hillside, there is a stopping place with a viewpoint and a plaque to President Lionel Fernández, during whose administration the road was built.

Getting around

Sánchez is the gateway town to the peninsula and a good road runs along the southern side of the peninsula to Samaná with a spur over the hills from Sánchez to Las Terrenas on the north side. There are good bus services from Santo Domingo and **Caribe Tours** uses the new toll road as one of its two routes. You can also get a ferry from Sabana de la Mar, across the bay.

Samaná → *For listings, see pages 79-85.*

The town of **Santa Bárbara de Samaná**, commonly known just as Samaná, is set in a protected harbour, within the Bahía de Samaná. Columbus arrived here on 12 January 1493, but was so fiercely repelled by the Ciguayo Indians that he called the bay the Golfo de las Flechas (Gulf of Arrows). Nowadays two small islets offshore are linked by a causeway to the mainland, providing a picturesque focal point when looking out to sea and added protection for yachts. The town itself is not startling, there are no colonial buildings, no old town to wander around, but the location is most attractive and it is a lively place particularly in whale-watching season.

Background
The present town of Santa Bárbara de Samaná was founded in 1756 by families expressly brought from the Canary Islands. The city, reconstructed after being devastated by fire in 1946, shows no evidence of this past, with its modern Catholic church, broad streets, new restaurants and hotels, and noisy rickshaw motorcycle taxis. Any remaining old buildings were torn down by Balaguer in the 1970s as part of his grand design to make the Samaná Peninsula into a huge tourist resort. When he was defeated in the 1978 elections his plans were discarded and Playa Dorada was developed instead. His dream is now being revived and the peninsula is witnessing an unprecedented construction boom with new hotels and villas, marina, golf course, airport, etc.

Places in Samaná
In contrast to the Catholic church, and overlooking it, is a more traditional Protestant church, white with red corrugated-iron roofing, nicknamed locally *La Churcha*. Its pulpit came from England, donated by the Methodist Church. They began the custom of holding harvest festivals, which still take place. The Malecón waterfront road is the main street in the town, lined with restaurants, bars and tour operators as well as a new and colourful complex of tourist shops, Pueblo Príncipe, close to the roundabout at the head of the bay. From the dock you can catch the ferry to Sabana de la Mar, some whale-watching tours and private yacht services. There are a couple of islands in the bay, linked by causeway from the luxury hotel, Gran Bahía Príncipe Cayacoa.

Humpback whales return to Samaná Bay at the beginning of every year to mate and calve. Various half-day tours go whale watching, certainly worthwhile if you are in the area then. This is recognized as one of the 10 best places in the world to see whales and is very convenient for the average tourist as they are so close to the shore. For more information on whales and whale watching, see box, page 77.

Samaná Peninsula → *For listings, see pages 79-85.*

Parque Nacional Los Haitises
ⓘ *Visits to the park can be arranged by launch, with departures from Samaná on the north side of the bay, and Sabana de la Mar on the south side. Permits must be obtained from the DNP, Sabana de la Mar, T809-556 7333.*

Across the bay is the Los Haitises National Park, a fascinating area of 208 sq km of mangroves, humid subtropical forest, seagrass beds, cays, *mogotes* and caves, which were used by the Taínos and later by pirates. The irregular topography of bumpy, green hills was caused by the uplifting of the limestone bedrock and subsequent erosion. There are anthropomorphic cave drawings and other pictures, best seen with a torch, and some carvings. Wooden walkways have been constructed through the caves and into the mangroves in a small area accessible to boats and tourists. The park is rich in wildlife and birds. Many of the caves have bats, but there are also manatee and turtles in the mangroves and inland the endangered solenodon. The *solenodonte*, or Hispaniolan solenodon (*Solenodon paradoxus*), is an insectivore with a long nose, round ears and long tail, with the appearance of a large rat, which grows to about 30 cm and can weigh 1 kg. It is the only mammal to inject venom out of its teeth like a snake and is a living fossil, having changed very little since it ran under the feet of dinosaurs 75 million years ago. It is critically endangered.

Various companies organize tours. Some include a trip upriver to a village and a swim in the Cristal lagoon (turquoise, cool, sweet water) as well as lunch on a beach near Sánchez. Take hats and lots of sun screen, no shade.

Cayo Levantado

The offshore island, Cayo Levantado, is popular, especially when a cruise ship is in or at weekends when the beach is packed and best avoided. The white-sand beach, known as **Bacardi Beach**, is nice, though, and there are good views of the bay and the peninsulas on either side. Unfortunately, a large hotel (**Gran Bahía Príncipe Cayo Levantado**) restricts access to the rest of the island. Public boats go there from the dock in Samaná (US$6-8 return, buy ticket at Malecón No 3, not from the hustlers on the pier, lots of boats daily); alternatively, take a *público* or *motoconcho* 8 km out of town to Los Cacaos (US$3) from where **Transportes José** and **Simi Báez** run boats to the island. Another option is to take a whale watching tour with Victoria Marine and for US$5 extra you can be dropped off at the beach for a few hours for lunch and sunbathing. There are restaurants and bars serving a fish lunch and drinks on the sand, expensive but you're paying for the location.

Las Galeras

At the eastern end of the peninsula is **Playa Galeras**. The 1-km beach is framed by the dark rock cliffs and forested mountains of **Cape Samaná** and **Cape Cabrón**, now designated a national park. The village is popular with Europeans, several of whom have set up small hotels and restaurants. There is a fair amount of weed on the beach and some coral, so rubber shoes are a good idea, but it is 'unimproved', with trees for shade. If you walk east along the beach you come to the hotel, **Grand Paradise Samana**, set among masses of coconut palms. The beach here is sandy with no coral and very safe for children.

Just before entering the village there is a turning to the left and a rough, dirt road leads to **La Playita**. A pretty spot with palm trees leaning at impossible angles towards the sea, the beach has a fine view of headlands along the peninsula. There is a restaurant on the sand, a dive shop, vendors, sunbeds and umbrellas for hire. It is on the cruise ship excursion schedule, but if there isn't a ship in Samaná Bay the beach is uncrowded and pleasant.

Playa Rincón is 20 minutes from Las Galeras by boat, US$10-15 return journey, or 40 minutes by jeep along a paved 8-km road to Rincón village, followed by a 2-km rocky and muddy track through coconut palms. Playa Rincón is dominated by the cliffs of 600-m high **Cape Cabrón** at one end but backed by thousands of coconut palms filling every available space. The sand is soft and there are few corals in the water, which is beautifully

Humpback whale

A fully grown humpback whale (*Megaptera novaeangliae*) measures 12-15 m and weighs 30-40 tonnes. It is dark grey, or black, with a white belly and long white flippers. On its nose and flippers it has large nodules, not perhaps an attractive feature, but the hairs coming out of the lumps on its nose are used like a cat uses its whiskers. All humpbacks can be identified by the markings on their tails, or flukes, as no two are the same, and scientists have recorded thousands of them so that they can trace and monitor them. They even give them names. Humpbacks are famous for their singing. Only the males sing and they all sing the same song, repeating phrases over and over again, sometimes for hours, but each year they have a new refrain, a variation on the theme, which they develop during the journey. Maybe to keep the kids amused along the way, but more likely to attract a mate. The humpback is a baleen whale, which means that it scoops up huge gulps of water containing small fish or krill, then sieves it, squeezing the water out between the baleens, retaining the food. When they are in the Bahía de Samaná, Banco Navidad (Navidad Bank) or the Banco de Plata (Silver Bank), they do not feed for the three months of their stay. The water is too warm to support their type of food, although a perfect temperature in which to give birth without harming the calf, which is born without any protective fat to ward off the cold. This fat is soon built up, however, in time for the return journey north to the western north Atlantic and Iceland, by drinking up to 200 litres a day of its mother's milk and putting on weight at a rate of 45 kg a day.

The Dominican Republic has the most popular and well established whale watching in the Caribbean. The industry is centred on humpback whales, but pilot whales and spotted dolphins can also be seen in Samaná Bay, and bottlenose, spinner and spotted dolphins, Bryde's and other whales on Silver Bank. The season for both locales is January through March with whale-watching tours in Samaná Bay 15 January to 15 March. Whale-watching trips in Samaná Bay last two to four hours. The trips to Silver Bank are more educational and are usually arranged by specialist groups offering tours of up to a week.

The whole of Samaná Bay, Silver Bank and Navidad Bank is now a National Marine Mammal Sanctuary. The aim is to include the peninsula and Los Haitises National Park and have it all declared a Biosphere Reserve by UNESCO. During the season the Dirección Nacional de Parques monitors the whale watching and has four vigilantes, recognizable by their green caps, of which three are in Samaná and one at Silver Bank. They can be contacted at the offices of the Centre for the Conservation and Ecodevelopment of Samaná Bay (CEBSE), T809-538 2042, www.samana.org.do/cebse-s.htm. A set of rules and guidelines has been drawn up by CEBSE, the DNP and the Association of Boat Owners in Samaná to regulate the activities of whale-watching boats, including limits on how close they can get to whales and how long they can remain watching them. Data has been collected on the impact on breeding of whale watching, to see if this new tourist attraction has been affecting the humpbacks. There has, however, been no change since 1987, with mothers and calves and singers still in the same area.

clear, but the beach is wild and uncleaned, so coconuts and branches litter the sand. On reaching the beach turn right along a track to get to several beach restaurants at the end where you can get delicious fried fish, caught that morning. They are on a small promontory which gives protection against the waves. This area has been bought for tourist development, but nothing has happened yet and it is still open to all.

Playa El Valle is reached by 10 km dirt road from Samaná, 4WD needed, or come by boat from Las Terrenas or Las Galeras. A *guagua* comes a couple of times a day from Samaná, US$1. Signs along this road will direct you to the Samaná Zipline, which takes in the Lulú waterfall where you can swim in the pool. The drive over the mountain is spectacularly beautiful, with two river crossings where women still wash their laundry and children hitch a ride to school. On the way back you get a wonderful view of the Samaná Bay with a flash of white sand on Cayo Levantado as you come over the top. The beach is undeveloped except for a tiny beach bar, where you can get a good fish lunch, but otherwise the beach is usually empty of tourists. The view from the beach is dramatic, with the headlands rising vertically out of the water and a river running into the sea. Coconut palms are everywhere, be careful about sitting underneath one for shade. Check before swimming at deserted beaches where there can be strong surf and an undertow. Drownings have occurred near El Valle. Only go in when the sea is flat calm, ask for advice at the beach bar or at the tiny naval station behind.

Las Terrenas

On the north coast of the peninsula is Las Terrenas, with some of the finest beaches in the country, from which, at low tide, you can walk out to coral reefs to see abundant sea life. The beaches go on for miles, fringed by palm trees under which are hidden a large number of small hotels and restaurants, often run by Europeans, attracted by the lifestyle. It is a quiet, low-key resort and never crowded, although development is in progress and greater numbers of visitors are expected; the beaches are mostly clean and remain beautiful. It is reached by a 17-km road from Sánchez which zig-zags steeply up to a height of 450 m with wonderful views before dropping down to the north coast. The road Samaná-Las Terrenas via Limón is also a pretty route although perhaps not so spectacular from the top. The new, toll road links Las Terrenas directly with the airport at El Catey and runs up into the hills along the northern coast behind the beaches for more spectacular views.

Las Terrenas is a busy and lively place which has grown rapidly over the last few years. In addition to a wealth of small and intimate places to stay, which is what brought tourists here in the first place, there are now lots of self-catering apartments, low-rise hotels, bars, restaurants and nightclubs. The beach is picture-book white sand, fringed with coconut palms stretching for some 5 km. At the end of the beach, walk behind a rocky promontory to reach **Playa Bonita**, with more hotels, guesthouses and restaurants, but quieter than Las Terrenas. Beyond the western tip of this beach is **Playa Cosón**, a magnificent 6-km arc of white sand and coconut groves ending in steep wooded cliffs (1½-hour walk or US$3 on *motoconcho*). A large all-inclusive hotel, **Viva Wyndham Samaná** (www.vivasamanaresort. com)is at the far end of Playa Cosón. A nice trip is to take a *motoconcho*, along a very bumpy dirt and sand track and walk back along the beach.

A right turn at the waterfront in Las Terrenas takes you about 4 km to the largest hotel in the area, **Gran Bahía Príncipe El Portillo** (www.bahia-principe.com), an all-inclusive resort. The currently disused airstrip is behind it on the other side of the road. **El Limón**, 10 km further on, is a farming village on the road across the peninsula to Samaná. From El Limón you can ride or hike for an hour into the hills to a 40-m-high waterfall on the Arroyo Chico and swim in a pool of green water at its foot. This is a popular excursion with cruise ship passengers as well as hotel guests, which means that the route has become well trampled and muddy, so riding certainly keeps your feet cleaner than hiking. The **Salto de Limón** (or Cascada del Limón) is a National Monument. There are four different access routes to the falls from the Samaná road, from the communities of Rancho Español, Arroyo Surdido, El Café and El Limón, from all of which you can hire horses, buy food and drinks and local produce. If taking a guide to the falls, fix the price in advance (the falls can be deserted, do not take valuables there). Access to the falls is regulated to prevent erosion and other damage; visits are only permitted during the day on foot or horseback. *Motoconcho* from Las Terrenas to El Limón US$2.50, but they will try to charge US$5-10.

Samaná Peninsula listings

For hotel and restaurant price codes and other relevant information, see pages 10-13.

⬤ Where to stay

Samaná *p75*
$$$$ Gran Bahía Príncipe Cayacoa, Loma Puerto Escondido, T809-538 3135, www.bahia-principe.com. Luxury all-inclusive overlooking the bay of Samaná, just before the causeway. Comfortable rooms and suites with glorious sea view from on high, elevator goes down hillside to beaches, 4 restaurants serving very good food, lots of activities and sports, very smart, efficient service.
$$ Chino, Calle San Juan 1, T809-538 2215. Up on the hill with a wonderful view over the town and bay, great for sunset watching. Well kept, immaculate rooms, best ones in newer part, pleasant service, only Spanish spoken. Very good Chinese restaurant.
$$ Samana Spring, Cristóbal Colón 94, 1 block from Malecón, T809-538 2946 (Spanish spoken), T829-763 2048 (English spoken). New, simple rooms but well equipped with comfy beds, efficient a/c and good bathrooms with hot water. Convenient location yet quiet. Helpful owner.
$ Backpackers Samaná (Cotubanamá), T809-538 3447, go west along the Malecón to the Pueblo Príncipe and the roundabout and turn right, the hotel is one block up on the left. Clean, adequate, rooms with 1-5 beds, a/c, fan, TV, Wi-Fi, basic kitchen at the back of the building.
$ Bahía View, Av Circunvalación 4, T809-538 3722. Up the hill from the roundabout and the Pueblo Príncipe, in walking distance of everywhere with view of bay. Restaurant downstairs, variety of rooms upstairs with fan or a/c, rooms facing the harbour have balconies, basic but OK for the price.

Las Galeras *p76*
Water is brackish here and you should not drink water from the tap. All hotels have salt-water showers.
$$$$-$$$ Chalet Tropical, Calle por La Playita, T809-901 0738, www.chalet tropical.com. 3 thatched cabañas sleeping 2-7 guests in a child-friendly garden with fruit trees and lawns. Each wood and stone rustic self-catering chalet is equipped with everything you need, including beach towels and drinking water. Host Sarah is phenomenally helpful and can arrange excursions and make recommendations. Excellent breakfast included.
$$$ Todo Blanco, T809-538 0201, www.hoteltodoblanco.com. Plantation house style, all white, gingerbread fretwork, 8 rooms with balconies overlooking the sea through palm trees, light and airy, good-sized bathrooms, gardens slope down to the beach. Breakfast available in dining room, on terrace or in your room, dinner by reservation only, outside restaurants will deliver. Tours available.
$$$ Villa Serena, T809-583 0000, www.villaserena.com. Plantation house theme with wooden balconies and verandas, overhanging roofs and a charming double staircase to the lobby. View across manicured gardens dotted with palms to the sea, where there is a tiny islet with a few palm trees. 21 elegant rooms, with a/c, ceiling fans. Drinking

water is provided. The restaurant offers European-style food, making its own pasta. Tours organized, free bicycles, kayaks, snorkel gear. Yoga and wellness retreat.

$$$-$$ El Marinique, T809-538 0262, www.elmarinique.com. 2 deluxe apartments, 3 cottages in delightful gardens with a path down to the sea.Cottages have 1 or 2 beds, a table and chairs, windows on all 4 sides for maximum ventilation and corrugated roofs. Apartments have a full kitchen, sofa bed in the living area and loft room upstairs, from where the balcony has a sea view. Nicole is a wonderful cook, see Restaurants. Boat trips to other beaches can be arranged on the beach, meal and activity packages available.

$$$-$$ Plaza Lusitania, T809-538 0093, www.plazalusitania.com. Suites and apartments for self-catering, spacious and comfortable, with tiled floors, a/c, fan. Conveniently located above the shops in the centre of the village, rooms facing the rear are quieter. Italian restaurant downstairs.

$$ Sol Azul, Calle Principal, T809-539 0001, www.elsolazul.com. Bed and breakfast, conveniently located for shops and beach. 4 rooms in individual thatched wooden cabañas in immaculate garden with pool. Double and bunk beds for families or couples. Mosquito nets on beds, no a/c. Very helpful owners, full of suggestions for what to do and where to go.

Las Terrenas *p78*

Hotels on the beach are more expensive than those behind them or inland.

$$$$ The Peninsula House, T809-962 7447, www.thepeninsulahouse.com. Old world elegance at this Victorian colonial house up on the hillside with glorious views of the ocean. On Condé Nast's Gold List of the world's best places to stay. 6 junior suites with terraces, no children. Manicured lawns and immaculate service. Lunch is at **The Beach Restaurant** (see below), breakfast and dinner at the hotel.

$$$$-$$$ Las Palmas al Mar, 27 de Febrero, about 1 km from town on Portillo road, T809-240 6292, www.laspalmasalmar. com. Great villas with 2 bedrooms, 2 bathrooms, veranda, rocking chairs, barbecue, all mod-cons and well stocked kitchens, Wi-Fi, large pool, beach towels, just across the road from a nice stretch of beach.

$$$$-$$$ Playa Colibrí, Francisco Caamaño Deñó 31, west end of Las Terrenas, T809-240 6434, www.hotelplayacolibri.com. 45 studios, 1-bedroom and 2-bedroom apartments, a few sleep 6-8, daily, weekly or monthly rates, kitchenette, pool, jacuzzi, parking, all clean and comfortable, sea view through the palm trees, breakfast on the beach, beach bar, friendly and helpful service.

$$$-$$ Albachiara, 27 de Febrero (Camino a Punto Popi), T809-240 5240, www. albachiarahotel.com. Just on the edge of town within easy walking distance of bars, shops and restaurants but quiet at night. Beach across the road. 1- to 3-bedroom apartments, spacious, comfortable and well cared for. Helpful service, breakfast included, pool, good for couples or families.

$$$-$$ Casa Nina, Av 27 de Febrero, Playa Popi, T809-240 5490, www.hotel-casanina.com. Turn right for 800 m along the beach in Las Terrenas in the direction of El Limón. Rooms, studios and apartments in cosy cabins painted in Caribbean colours around pool in gardens. Nice spot facing the sea. Bar for snacks and drinks by the beach, restaurant in garden for meals.

$$ Casas del Mar Neptunia, 1 Emilio Prud'homme, T809-240 6884, www. casasdelmarneptunia.com. 10 rooms in colourful bungalows in garden with breakfast, fan and fridge, hot water, good value, convenient for beach and town, friendly service, helpful staff, Jim and Suzanne speak English.

$ Fata Morgana, off Fabio Abreu, inland between Las Terrenas and Playa Bonita, T809-836 5541, www. fatamorganalasterrenas.com. Long-time resident, Edit de Jong, runs this sociable hostel for people who want to be comfortable but not pampered. 6 rooms with bathroom sleep 1-4, fan, each room has veranda with rocking chairs and hammock. Communal kitchen and dining area, book exchange, barbecue area, large garden with donkeys, dogs and other animals, parking, quiet place away from the beach. Shops and a bakery around the corner, motoconcho into town US$1.25 daytime, US$2.50 at night, or rent a moto for US$20 per day.

Playa Bonita *p78*

Playa Bonita is quieter than Las Terrenas but within easy reach if you want nightlife or shops in town.

$$$ Acaya, Playa Bonita, T809-240 6161, www.hotel-acaya-fr.com. 2 buildings on the beach, 16 rooms all with ocean view, fan, a/c, terrace, good breakfast included, thatched restaurant, international menu, no credit cards. Surf club on site.

$$$ Atlantis, T809-240 6111, www.atlantis-hotel.com.do. French-run, delightful beach hotel, known for its excellent French cuisine, chef Gérard used to work for President Mitterrand. Lawns and garden run to the sand under coconut palms, white curvaceous architecture reminiscent of Mediterranean styles, 18 spacious rooms, all different sizes and decor, some with a/c, breakfast and taxes included, pleasant beachfront bar with swinging chair. perfect for sunset watching. One of the nicest hotels in the country.

$$$-$$ Coyamar, 1st hotel at Playa Bonita, T809-240 5130, www.coyamar.com. German-run, 10 simply furnished rooms in 2 buildings, the nicest ones are upstairs with veranda, cosy, beachfront, friendly, helpful, good bar and restaurant. Very nice garden with small pool.

🍴 Restaurants

Samaná *p75*

The local cuisine is highly regarded, especially the fish and coconut dishes and *sancocho*.

$$$ Café del Mar Puerto Bahía, Paseo de la Marina, T829-465211, www.cafedelmar.com.do. 1130-late. An offshoot of the original **Café del Mar** in Ibiza, this indoor/outdoor restaurant in the new, private marina, Puerto Bahía, is chic and stylish, boasting a view of both sunrise and sunset and offering good, international dishes, tapas, sandwiches, burgers and cocktails. Comfortable sun beds and loungers on the deck, small pool, good music.

$$$ La Mata Rosada, opposite the harbour, T809-538 2388. 1200-2300. French-run but lots of languages spoken, popular with expats, fish and seafood is excellent, prepared many ways and always tasty and interesting.

$$$ L'Hacienda, Malecón, T809-538 2383. Thu-Tue 1200-late. Grill and bar open from 1200, the best in town, excellent specials. French chef José cooks delectable steaks and seafood on the grill.

$$$-$$ Bahía Azul, Malecón, T809-538 2694. Local and not-so-local food, outdoor seating under umbrellas for shade, good for a pleasant lunch with a cold beer watching the boats.

$$$-$$ Taberna Mediterranea, Malecón, T829-994 3634. Spanish taberna style overlooking the waterfront and the boats. Known for the surf and turf plate for 2, which is enough for 4.

$$-$ Le Royal Snack, Malecón, T829-994 2952. On the waterfront between Caribe Tours and Orange. French Yvon and Nathalie offer real croissants and espresso for breakfast as well as other pastries, sandwiches, grilled chicken, burgers and French fries, all very tasty. New and clean with good bathrooms.

Las Galeras *p76*

Locals eat at the *mini-comedores* on the beach at the end of the road where the *guaguas* stop, not recommended for hygiene but plenty of local colour. You can find boatmen here for trips to other beaches.

$$$ Le Tainos, T829-713 7463, www.letainos.com. In the centre of the village on the main street, thatched conical building in Taíno style housing a smart restaurant and bar. French owners, stylish food artfully served on large square plates, rice comes in a coconut shell, fish is cooked in a banana leaf. Popular, good atmosphere with excellent cocktails.

$$$-$$ Chez Denise, Carr Samaná, T809-538 0219. Open 1030-2330. French food, delicious crêpes, shrimp, salads. Colourful and friendly.

$$$-$$ El Cabito, La Caleta, T829-697 9506, info@elcabito.net. Perched on a bluff, this restaurant has the best view on the island although it is a bit tricky to get to. Go for lunch in whale watching season and you can see humpbacks just offshore. At night it is a romantic spot. The food is excellent and very good value.

$$$-$$ El Pescador, Calle Principal, T809-538 0052. Wed-Mon 1400-late. On your right as you head out of the village, look for the coloured lights and the building painted terracotta, blue and white. Spanish-owned, specializes in seafood (good paella), fish, shrimp, lobster and crab accompanied by small salad and rice. Also has wood oven for pizza.

$$$-$$ Nicole's Ocean View Restaurant, El Marinique, T809-538 0262, www.el marinique.com. Breakfast, lunch and dinner. Delicious papaya crêpes, seafood caught daily and delicious home-made desserts. Nicole bakes her own bread and pastries. Also good steaks and barbecue lobster, chicken and ribs, all served on shady outdoor veranda by the bar overlooking the sea.

Las Terrenas *p78*

Las Terrenas has hundreds of restaurants to choose from, in town, on the beaches or tucked away on back streets. Most of them are good and the fish is fresh. The **Pueblo de los Pescadores** (fishermen's village) is a collection of new, colourful wooden buildings in typical Caribbean style on the waterfront. They have replaced the old fishermen's huts converted to restaurants which burned down. There are bars, tapas bars, burger bars and restaurants of many varieties, so it is worth walking along to see which takes your fancy. Entered from the road, they all open out on to

the sand with decking and verandas and are a focal point for nightlife with music, dancing and other entertainment.

$$$ Mi Corazón, Juan Pablo Duarte 7, esq Carr Playa Bonita, T809-240 5329, www. micorazon.com. Open from 1900 Tue-Sun Nov-Apr, Tue-Sat May-Sep. Swiss hosts, innovative German chef, the best place in the area for fine dining with beautiful food and attentive, multilingual service. Exceptional tasting menu if you can't make up your mind. Local and organic ingredients are used where possible, delicious sorbets and other extra titbits add to the enjoyment of the meal. Upstairs above a bakery, the restaurant is in elegant Spanish courtyard style with a water feature on the end wall and the patio open to the night sky, while the tables are through arches around the edge. On the top floor is a bar and lounge for after dinner. Great for a special evening.

$$$ The Beach Restaurant, Playa Cosón, T809-847 3288, see Facebook. Lunch until 1700. The beach club for **The Peninsula House**. A charming gingerbread cottage with lawns running down to the sea. Elegant dining, Caribbean-style, with wicker chairs and staff all in white. Excellent food and drinks, a special place, if a bit difficult to find. Sun beds and beach towels for guests; go for the afternoon, showers available after you've been to the beach.

$$ Casa Coco, 27 de Febrero, T809-499 6076. Open 1200-2400. The first pizzeria to open in town and still good, with a restaurant or home delivery for an extra charge. Pizzas made Italian style with lots of toppings to choose from.

$$ Luis, Playa Cosón. Ramshackle beach bar at Cosón where you can get a delicious, typical seafood lunch of freshly grilled fish or other seafood accompanied by rice, beans, tostones, salad, washed down with a chilled beer or piña colada. Plastic tables and chairs on the sand, some in shade, musicians sometimes serenade you while you eat.

$$ Mojitos, Punta Popi, T809-284 0337, see Facebook. Pleasant restaurant, bar, lounge with tables on covered wooden deck above the sand. Cuban, local and international food such as burgers or fried chicken. The place for mojito lovers, with other flavours such as passionfruit and tamarind to try. Sunset happy hour 1730-1930. You can rent sunbeds from them for a day on the beach.

$$ Pacomer, Libertad, behind the cemetery on the beach. A seafood lunch spot with plastic tables and chairs on the sand right by where fishermen bring in their catch. Paco speaks French, English and Spanish and serves up a variety of delicious dishes with a French twist.

$$ Spoon Beach, Fco Alberto Caamaño, Residencia Bonita Village, Playa Las Ballenas, T809-884 9971. Chef Willy runs this highly regarded restaurant in the gardens of a rental apartment complex at the west end of Las Terrenas where the river joins the sea. Excellent fish, French and Vietnamese dishes, delicious desserts, all very good value.

🍸 Bars and clubs

Samaná *p75*
Outdoor nightlife can be found along the Malecón, where several stalls are set up as bars at weekends and fiestas. There is usually music at one or other of the restaurants, whether live or recorded. Nightclubs open and close sporadically and many are little more than brothels.

Las Terrenas *p78*
At weekends there is quite a lot going on, particularly along the beach road, with street sellers of food and drinks and impromptu drum music. There is often music at the bars and restaurants for gentle entertainment. There are several bars at the Pueblo de los Pescadores, while on the other side of the road is **Gaia**, a club on 3 floors, noticeable for its plentiful use of neon. **Son Latino** on the main street is a good dance place. **Bombú** car wash at the fuel station is a local place for music and dancing. **La Bodega**, by the cemetery, is where locals and tourists meet

up for dancing: an open-air bar and dance space in the plaza by the seafront.

🎉 Festivals

Samaná *p75*
Traditional dances, such as *bambulá* and the *chivo florete*, can be seen at local festivals.
4 Dec Patron saint's day.
24 Oct San Rafael.

🏊 What to do

Samaná *p75*
Diving
H2O & Ozeanic Caribbean, Malecón, T829-569 5512, www.diving-watersports.com, T829-650 0572, www.ozeanic-caribbean.com. 2 companies in one with Dutch and German management and multilingual staff. Courses and dives offered in the Bay of Samaná and around Las Galeras. Also snorkelling, deep-sea fishing and land-based excursions.

Whale watching
All tours mid-Jan to mid-Mar, depending on when the whales actually arrive and depart the Bay. Only take tours with licensed operators. Their vessels will have a Ministry of the Environment white flag with a permit number (1-43) on it and the same number will be on the hull. There are strict regulations they all have to follow so as not to harass the whales.
Transporte Marítimo Minadiel, T809-538 2556, minadiel@yahoo.com. Their small boats can get close but have a restricted view of the whales.
Whale Samaná, Victoria Marine, T809-538 2494, www.whalesamana.com. Kim Beddall runs excellent tours in a large boat giving a good view, with hydrophone, US$50 plus US$3 marine park fee. Multilingual naturalist guides explain what is happening and answer questions. A thrill for anyone, especially children (US$25). Seasickness pills offered and recommended. Life jackets and rain gear on board. Optional visit to Cayo Levantado after whale watching, US$5.

Tour operators

Amilka Tours, T809-552 7664, www.amilka toursdr.com. Known for their boat tours to Los Haitises National Park, but they also do whale watching and trips to Cayo Levantado. **Tour Samaná With Terry**, T809-538 3179, see Facebook. Lots of day trips and activities including ziplining, waterfalls, Los Haitises, popular with cruise visitors in particular.

Las Galeras *p76*
Diving

Las Galeras Divers, Plaza Lusitania, T809-538 0220, www.las-galeras-divers.com. Swiss owners, multilingual staff, boat dives for all levels of divers, PADI courses offered. A single dive is US$45, a double dive US$75, plus US$10 for equipment, lower prices for dive packages. Dive sites around Cabo Samaná and Cabo Cabrón, including coral gardens, wreck diving, caves, canyons and cliffs.

Las Terrenas *p78*
Diving

See also page 41.
Turtle Dive Center, Centro Comercial, El Paseo de la Costanera, T829-903 0659, www.turtledivecenter.com. Philippe and Corinne offer SSI courses for all levels. Introductory dives are US$65, while for divers with certification, a single dive is US$60 and 2-tank dives US$100, all equipment included.

Tour operators

La Casa de las Terrenas, Calle Principal 280, opposite Plaza Taína, T809-240 6251, www.lasterrenas-excursions.com. Stephanie, French naturalist, specialises in Los Haitises and whalewatching tours but also offers the standard tours to Cayo Levantado, Salto Limón, quad bike tours etc.

⊖ Transport

Samaná *p75*
Air

Prof Juan Bosch at El Catey (AZS), T809-338 5888 to the west of the peninsula on the north coast, is the international airport for the area. There are flights with **Air Canada**, **Air Transat**, **WestJet**, **JetBlue**, **Sunwing**, **Condor**, **LTU**, **Corsair Fly**, and **Thompson UK**. Taxi from the airport is US$70 to **Santa Bárbara de Samaná**, US$93 to **Las Terrenas** and US$100 to **Las Galeras**. Arroyo Barril airport, just west of Samaná on the southern coast, receives daily flights from Punta Cana with **Aerodomca**, US$150. There is also an airstrip east of Las Terrenas at El Portillo, but it was closed for repairs in 2012 which have not been carried out.

Boat

There is a ferry 4 times a day across the bay from Sabana de la Mar to Samaná taking foot passengers only. Morning crossings are usually calmer than the afternoon, when the sea can be choppy. Many yachts anchor at Samaná. The Port Captain comes on board when you arrive, with a group of officials, each of whom may expect a tip to expedite the paperwork. It can be particularly bad at weekends and holidays. Cruise ships come into Samaná Bay, including **Norwegian Cruise Line**, **Royal Caribbean**, **Holland America** and **Oceania Cruises**. There are plans to build a cruise port.

Bus and taxi

For short excursions you can take a *motoconcho*, some of which have been fitted with tricycles like rickshaws. There are also *guaguas*, or minibuses, for a safer ride. *Concho* or *guagua* in town US$0.30; *carreras* US$3.50-4. *Guagua* to Sánchez from market place US$2.50. *Guaguas* from Sánchez and Samaná to Las Galeras run every 30 mins until 1800.

From the capital the quickest route is via the new toll road. **Caribe Tours** has 2 routes to Samaná: either from their Las Américas Expressway terminal at the entry to the Autopista del Nordeste toll road (2½ hrs), 10 mins from the airport (airport taxi US$20 to the bus station), leaving 0830, 1030, 1500, 1700, US$8; or from their main terminal on 27 de Febrero in Santo Domingo

(4 hrs), leaving 0700, 0930, 1430, 1630, via Nagua. Both buses stop at Sánchez to drop off travellers to Las Terrenas. **Transporte Samaná – Asotrapusa**, Calle Barahona 129, or terminal at Las Américas Expressway, T809-687 1470 in Santo Domingo, T829-222 0368 in Samaná, leaves at 0830, 0930, 1100, 1340, 1500 from Santo Domingo, returning 0500, 0700, 0900, 1400, 1500 from near the cemetery in Las Terrenas, US$7.50-9. Buses via the toll road to Las Terrenas leave at 1130 and 1405. They also have buses at 0630, 0800 and 1230 to Las Galeras with a stopover in Sánchez and Samaná. Alternatively from the capital by bus or *público* to San Pedro de Macorís, then another to **Sabana de la Mar** and take the ferry across the bay.

Road

Toll roads are the quickest, shortest and safest, with the least traffic, but they are expensive. From Santo Domingo, head east on the Autopista Las Américas (US$0.75 on the way out, free on the return) then take the Autopista del Nordeste heading north, a few minutes after Las Américas international airport, 1½ hrs. The speed limit is 80 kph and the road is patrolled by police cars. There are several toll booths, all charging different amounts, so take plenty of small change as they do not accept RD$2000 bills. In 2013, Peaje Naranjal was US$4 and Peaje Guaraguao US$4.75, while the toll road from Catey airport to Las Terrenas was US$11.25. To avoid tolls, you can drive from Santo Domingo up the Autopista Duarte (100 kph), then take the road Cotuí-Pimentel-Castillo-Factor-Nagua-Sánchez-Samaná, which will take you about twice as long.

From Punta Cana, take the Autopista del Coral via La Romana, then the Autovía del Este towards Las Américas airport, 2 hrs, turning north to the Autopista del Nordeste, 2 hrs.

Las Galeras p76
Bus

Las Galeras is 1 hr, US$2.50 by *guagua*, from either the market or the dock in Samaná. All transport congregates where the road ends at the beach, by the *comedores* on the sand. *Guaguas* leave when more or less full but you won't have to wait long.

Las Terrenas p78
Bus and taxi

Motoconchos whizz up and down the road through the village and weave their way along the beach track, US$1-5, depending on how far you go.

Caribe Tours stops in **Sánchez** (T809-552 7434) on the way to **Samaná**, from Santo Domingo. You will be met by *motoconchos*, US$5 to the *guagua* stop in Las Terrenas, up to US$7.50 to a hotel further along the beach. A taxi (minibus) Sánchez-Las Terrenas costs US$25. Note that *guaguas* which meet arriving **Caribe Tours** buses in Sánchez overcharge for the journey to Las Terrenas. **Transporte Samaná – Asotrapusa** (see above) runs from Santo Domingo to Las Terrenas via Samaná.

Car

Lots of car, jeep, *moto* hire. Motorbikes (US$20-25) and mountain bikes (no brakes) can be hired. Jeep rental US$60-90. There is a petrol/gasoline station.

❶ Directory

Samaná p75
Medical services Centro Médico de Especialidades Samaná (CMES), Coronel Andrés Díaz 6, T809-538 3999, www.cmes.com. 24-hr emergency, X-rays, ultrasound, laboratory, pharmacy, French and English translators available.

Las Galeras p76
Medical services Centro Médico Las Galeras, main road, T809-538 0134, lasgaleras@cmes.com.do.

East to Punta Cana

The eastern end of the island is generally flatter and drier than the rest, although the hills of the Cordillera Oriental are attractive and provide some great views. Cattle and sugar cane are the predominant agricultural products and this is definitely cowboy country. However, much of the sugar land has been turned over to more prosperous activities such as tourism, the Casa de Campo development being a prime example. The main beach resorts are Boca Chica, Juan Dolio, Casa de Campo, Bayahibe, Punta Cana and Bávaro, but there are several other smaller and more intimate places to stay.

Along the southeast coast → *For listings, see pages 92-95.*

Boca Chica

About 25 km east of Santo Domingo is the beach town of Boca Chica, the principal resort for the capital. Its days of being a quiet fishing village are long gone. It is set on a reef-protected shallow lagoon, with a wide sweep of white sand and the water is perfect for families. At weekends and holidays the beach is heaving with people. Tourist development has been intensive and there are many hotels, aparthotels and restaurants of different standards with lots of bars and rather seedy nightlife. Vendors line the main road, selling mostly Haitian paintings of poor quality but they are colourful. At weekends you can get freshly fried fish and *yaniqueques* (Johnny cakes) from the *fritureras* along the beach. There are numerous small bars and restaurants all along Calle Duarte, the main road, which is closed to traffic at night and restaurants move their tables on to the streeet. Restaurants stay open until around 2300 and a family atmosphere prevails. From around 0200 hotel and restaurant workers show up and by 0300 everything is in full swing, finally winding down around 0400. Under-age prostitution and drugs are a constant problem.

Juan Dolio

Guayacanes, Embassy and Juan Dolio beaches, east of Boca Chica, are also popular, especially at weekends when they can be littered and plagued with hawkers (much cleaner and very quiet out of season). The whole area is being developed in a long ribbon of holiday homes, hotels and resorts, and the new highway has improved access. **Guayacanes** has a nice little beach and the village is less overcrowded than Boca Chica. Buses going along the south coast will drop you, and pick you up again, at the various turn-offs to the beaches. **Juan Dolio** village is growing, with hotels, apartments, restaurants and bars, a tour agency and dive shop. This is the only beach in the country to allow high-rise buildings. East of Juan Dolio is the resort of **Villas del Mar**, and the beach area of **Playa Real**, with all-inclusive resorts and several apartment developments. Standards are not high in this area, many of the hotels are in need of refurbishment and service is often lacking. A night or two on arrival or prior to departure is probably enough. There are many, much nicer places to stay in the country and, if you want a beachfront all-inclusive, Punta Cana is better.

Reserva Antropológica de las Cueva de las Maravillas

① T809-696 1797, Tue-Sun 1000-1800, US$10, taxi from La Romana US$20.

The Reserva Antropológica de las Cueva de las Maravillas, at Cumayasa, 15 km after San Pedro de Macorís on the way to La Romana (signed off main road through a grand entrance with white fencing along the road), is excellent and well worth a detour off the main road. The huge caves are now managed by the Ministry of the Environment and access is regulated. There are walkways, steps and ramps through the caves and a discreet lighting system works on sensors. You walk down 140 steps but return via an elevator. The elevator sometimes breaks down, and in any case does not get you all the way up at the end of the tour, you still need to climb a bit, but other than that the attraction works well and is clean and tidy with pleasant gardens planted outside. Inside the caves there are stalactites, stalagmites and Taíno cave drawings. A knowledgeable guide will accompany you on your one-hour tour and answer questions. There's a museum, shop, cafeteria, toilets and facilities for wheelchair users. Photography only by prior arrangement.

La Romana

East of San Pedro de Macorís is La Romana. Parts of the road between the two towns are dual carriageway and they are working on the rest, but still watch out for cows on the road. A bypass was being built around La Romana town in 2013, but in the meantime it is a slow drive through the town centre. The town is dominated by its sugar factory, which can be seen all along the coast. There are still railways here which carry sugar to the Central La Romana and the trains' horns can be heard through the night. The town is very spread out, mostly on the west bank of the Río Dulce, which reaches the sea here. Cruise ships come in to the mouth of the river by the bridge. On the way east out of town is an enormous free trade zone, Zona Franca, which, contains the largest cigar factory in the world, among other factories. The Río Chavón area east of La Romana and Casa de Campo is a protected zone to safeguard a large area of red and black mangroves.

Isla Catalina

Off La Romana is Monumento Natural Isla Catalina (also called **Serena Cay**). Although inland the southeast part of the island is dry, flat and monotonous, the beaches have fine white sand. The reef provides protected bathing and excellent diving. Tours come from all the eastern resorts. Cruise ships also call, disgorging some 100,000 passengers in a winter season. The island is under the permanent supervision of the Dominican Navy and the Ministry of Tourism. All works that may affect the vegetation have been prohibited.

Casa de Campo

Just east of La Romana you join the Coral Highway, from where it is 4 km to La Romana international airport. You pass the entrance to Casa de Campo, the premier tourist centre in the Republic. Many famous people have stayed here, including Michael Jackson and Lisa Marie Presley when they got married in the Dominican Republic in 1994. Bill Clinton is a regular visitor and Julio Iglesias has a house here. The resort was built in 1974 by Charles Bluhdorn, the founder of **Gulf & Western**, which originally grew sugar cane on the land. After he died the Cuban-American family Fanjul bought it and opened it to paying guests in the 1980s. It is kept isolated from the rest of the country behind strict security. Covering 7000 acres, it is vast, exclusive, with miles of luxury villas surrounded by beautifully tended gardens full of bougainvillea and coleus of all colours. It has won numerous awards and accolades from travel and specialist sporting magazines. A **Marina and Yacht Club** with

Customs on site is at the mouth of the Río Chavón, from where you can take boat trips up the river. Cruise ships also call here.

Sport is the key to the resort's success. There are lots of activities on offer and they are all done professionally and with no expense spared. The tennis club has 13 courts where you can have lessons with a pro or knock up with a ballboy; the club is busy from early in the morning to late at night. The riding school has some 150 horses for polo, showjumping, trail riding, or whatever you want to do. The polo is of a particularly high standard and international matches are held here. For those with a keen eye, there is a world-class Sporting Clays facility developed by the British marksman, Michael Rose, with trap, skeet and sporting clays. Above all, however, guests come here for the golf. There are three world-class 18-hole courses designed by Pete Dye: 'The Links', 'Teeth of the Dog' and the most recent 'Dye Fore', a hilly course on the banks of the Río Chavón. The Teeth of the Dog, ranked number one in the Caribbean, has seven water holes which challenge even the greatest players.

Altos de Chavón

Altos de Chavón is an international artists' village in mock-Italian style built by an Italian cinematographer, in a spectacular hilltop setting above the gorge through which flows the Río Chavón. Students from all over the world come to the art school, but the village is now a major tourist attraction and is linked to **Casa de Campo**. There are several restaurants of a variety of nationalities, expensive shops and a disco. The **Church of St Stanislaus**, finished in 1979 and consecrated by Pope John Paul II, contains the ashes of Poland's patron saint and statue from Krakow. It is a perfect spot for a wedding with a lovely view of the river and great photo opportunities. An amphitheatre for open-air concerts seating 5500 was inaugurated with a show by Frank Sinatra (many international stars have performed there, from Julio Iglesias to Gloria Estefan and the best Dominican performers). There is also an excellent little **Museo Arqueológico Regional** ① *T809-523 8554, www.altosdechavon.museum*, with explanations in Spanish and English and lots of information about the Taínos.

Bayahibe and around → *For listings, see pages 92-95.*

Bayahibe

Bayahibe is a fishing village (about 25 km east of La Romana) on a small bay in a region of dry tropical forest and cactus on the edge of the **Parque Nacional del Este**, a great place to stay, with excursions, diving, budget lodgings and cafés. Recent archaeological discoveries have shown that there were groups of hunter-gatherers living in the Bayahibe area around 2000 BC and that later immigrants arriving around 1500 BC used pottery, made weights for their fishing nets and tools from conch and coral to grate foods. Its proximity to the park and offshore islands has made it popular with divers and it is considered one of the best dive destinations in the country. Small wooden houses and church of the village are on a point between the little bay and an excellent, 1.5 km curving white-sand beach fringed with palms. For a guided tour of the area contact the **Tourist Information Centre** ① *Plaza Montecarlo, Carr Dominicus esq Av Wayne Fuller, T829-520 9154, www.explorelaromana. com, open daily 0900-1700.* There are lots of rooms and cabañas to rent and several bars and restaurants for low-budget travellers but all-inclusive resorts now dominate the area. Plenty of fishing and pleasure boats are moored in the bay and it is from here that boats depart for Isla Saona.

Isla Saona

Isla Saona is a picture book tropical island with palm trees and white sandy beaches, set in a protected national park. However it is also an example of mass tourism, which conflicts with its protected status. Every day some 1000 tourists are brought on catamarans, speed boats or smaller *lanchas*, for a swim, a buffet lunch with rum on the beach and departure around 1500 with a stop off at the 'swimming pool' a patch of waist-deep water on a sand bank, where more rum is served. The sea looks like rush hour when the boats come and go. If you arrange a trip independently on a *lancha*, a smaller, slower boat, the local association of boat owners assures uniform prices.

Parque Nacional del Este

The Parque Nacional del Este (430 sq km) is on the peninsula south of San Rafael de Yuma between the villages of Bayahibe and Boca de Yuma and includes the Isla Saona, Isla Catalina and Isla Catalinita. It is a combination of subtropical humid forest, dry forest and transitional forest between the two, with a large number of endemic trees. The peninsula was formed about one million years ago out of marine rocks formed into terraces by the waves. Pockets of soil have been deposited between the rocks and the land is highly porous with no rivers. It has remote beaches and is the habitat of the now scarce *paloma Coronita* (crowned or white-headed dove, *Columba leucocephala*), the rhinocerous iguana and of various turtles. Some 112 species of bird have been registered here, of which eight are endemic to the island and 11 endemic to the Caribbean. As well as the crowned dove there are the Hispaniolan parrot, red-footed boobies, barn owls, stygian owls, brown pelicans and frigate birds. The solenodon and the hutia have been found here and marine mammals include the manatee and the bottlenose dolphin (*Tursiops truncates*). The geology of the area has created a number of caves, many of which are believed to be linked in an underground tunnel system. Some of the caves contain pre-Columbian pictographs (drawings) and petrographs (carvings), particularly in the eastern part of Guaraguao. You can visit the **Cueva de Berna** ⓘ *daily 0900-1600, US$2.50*, which contains around 300 drawings.

Diving Wear shoes when you go in the water as there is broken glass. Some of the best diving in the country is in this area, in the national park, and although local fishermen are still spearfishing, the reef is in good condition and there are plenty of fish, more in some areas than others. Dolphins are often seen from the boat, while underwater you find sharks and rays off Catalinita Island, east of Saona, reef sharks at La Parguera, west of Saona, the wreck of *St George* close to the *Dominicus* and freshwater caves inland for experienced divers. For dive operators, see page 94.

Higüey and around → *For listings, see pages 92-95.*

Higüey

The main town in the far east of the island is the modern, dusty and concrete Higüey. The **Basílica de Nuestra Señora de la Altagracia** (patroness of the Republic) can be seen for miles away. It is a very impressive modern building, to which every year there is a pilgrimage on 21 January; the statue of the Virgin and a silver crown are in a glass case on the altar and are paraded through the streets at the end of the fiesta. According to legend, the Virgin appeared in 1691 in an orange tree to a sick girl. Oranges are conveniently in season in January and huge piles of them are sold on the streets, while statues made of orange wood are also in demand. The Basilica was started by Trujillo in 1954, but finished by Balaguer in 1972. The architects were French, the stained glass is French. The Italian bronze doors (1988) portray the history of the Dominican Republic.

South of Higüey, east of Bayahibe, 1 km outside San Rafael de Yuma, is the **Casa de Ponce de León** ① *daily 0900-1600, US$1.25*. Juan Ponce de León, who was on Columbus' second voyage from Spain, was in charge of the military campaign which conquered the Higüey *cacicazgo* in 1507 and he was made lieutenant governor of Higüey by Governor Nicolás de Ovando. He took over the Indians' agricultural holdings and maintained a prosperous hacienda which helped to finance his later explorations of the Americas. The Casa de Ponce de León is an important historical landmark, one of the oldest fortified houses (*casa fortaleza*), built in 1505-1508 by Indian slaves. It is known locally as Las Ruinas, but in fact it has been restored and is in excellent health. This tall, square, stone mini-fortress has two floors with a tiled roof. There are very few windows and those are designed for defence. Large wooden doors face away from the approach to the house, which is set in pleasant gardens. Inside there is some mahogany furniture, a bed, a desk and some items supposedly belonging to Ponce de León. A tunnel for a quick escape used to run a long way underground into what is now a sugar cane field.

Punta Cana

Punta Cana, on the coast due east from Higüey, has some beautiful beaches, good diving and other watersports, excellent golf courses and an international airport. The area is not particularly pretty, the land is flat and the vegetation is mostly scrub and cactus, except for the palm trees along the beach. For many years there were only two resorts. The **Club Med** opened in 1981, followed by the **Punta Cana Beach Resort** in 1988 and a golf course runs between them. Since then there has been a construction boom, with new hotels or villa developments with marinas, golf courses and other facilities. There is even a championship bowling alley in the residential area, with 18 lanes, billiards, internet and cafeteria. Independent visitors find it difficult to find a public beach as the hotels will not allow non-residents through their property. The best beach to head for is **Juanillo**, at Cap Cana, where there is an excellent beach bar/restaurant of the same name (**$$$**), a wide expanse of bright, white sand, palm trees, hammocks and clear, turquoise water.

Bávaro

Continuing round the coast, there are many other beaches with white sand and reef-sheltered water. The area now known as Bávaro was once a series of fishing villages, but they have disappeared under the weight of hotels which contrast with the shacks still hanging on in places. All the hotels are usually booked from abroad as package holidays and most of them are all-inclusive, run by international companies.

Playa el Cortecito is a little oasis, a breath of fresh air in amongst the all-inclusives, being the nearest thing to a village that you will find on this stretch of coast. Here and in the neighbouring **Los Corales**, there are several beach bars, restaurants, gift shops, a supermarket, watersports and tour operators. It is a lively place and makes a welcome change from the all-inclusive life style.

Bibijagua is more of a craft market than anything else, with restaurants and bars. The Mercado Artesanal, cleverly signed as BI²JH²O, is a large covered market on the beach where you can buy handicrafts, rum, cigars (likely to be fakes), T-shirts, paintings (copies of Haitian art) and other souvenirs; but don't buy the shell, turtles and stuffed sharks which are for sale, as they are protected by international treaties and should be impounded by customs officials on your return home.

A road runs west from Higüey to Hato Mayor, via El Seibo, passing through hilly cattle and agricultural land. It is 43 km from Higüey to El Seibo and the road is most attractive through the foothills of the Cordillera Oriental. The 'living fences' are covered in pink blossom in January. You will see sugar cane fields with oxen, trains, *bateyes* where the cutters live and much poverty. There are lots of little villages where you can stop for snacks and fruit.

El Seibo is a quiet little town with painted houses, like many others in the region. It has a lovely 16th-century church, the first to be built in the east, with a beautiful brick dome and well-preserved brick ceiling. Doña Manuela Diez de Duarte, the mother of Juan Pablo Duarte, was born here and there is a statue to her outside the church. Sunday is a big day for cockfighting and you will often see people practising with their birds on the roadside or grooming their prize fighters. Note that a chicken, or cockerel for the pot, will be carried upside down and held by the feet to stop it squawking, but a fighting cock is held lovingly upright along one arm and caressed to calm him. The **Santa Cruz de Mayo** fiesta in the first full week in May involves bullfighting every evening at the rodeo in town. Despite the presence of professional *matadores*, there is no kill, although the bulls are tormented to the point of exhaustion.

Miches, 37 km north of El Seibo, is on the coast, reached by a pretty, twisty road over the mountains. From the top of the hill you can see across to Samaná, lovely views down to the coast with the changing colours of the sea. The soil is very red up here and white chickens turn orange from scratching in the dirt. Miches can also be reached from Bávaro on a coastal road, which is being improved as tourist development of the east spreads. The beach at Miches is wild, unimproved and stretches for miles.

Hato Mayor is 23 km west of El Seibo, a pretty drive through more hilly cattle country. It is an important junction for routes north-south between Sabana de la Mar on the north coast (ferry to Samaná) and San Pedro de Macorís on the south coast, and east to Higüey. It is a dusty town with not much to recommend it other than its transport links. West of the town, however, is one of the area's leading tourist attractions. Take the Yerba Buena road and after 32 km on a paved road you come to **Rancho Capote**, on which is the **Cueva Fun Fun** (pronounced foon foon) ① *Duarte 12, Barrio Puerto Rico, Hato Mayor del Rey, T809-299 0457, www.cuevafunfun.net, booked through a tour agency or independently.* This is a great excursion, not to be missed, involving horse riding, rappelling, scrambling along a cave through which a river runs and in which you will see stalactites, stalagmites and bats. There is even Taíno rock art at the mouth of the cave. The guides are helpful, supportive and fun, enabling everyone to participate, whatever their fitness levels.

At the east end of **Parque Nacional Los Haitises**, is **Sabana de la Mar**, the ferry port for boats to Samaná across the Bahía de Samaná. The area is the focus of some tourism development, with roads being built and a hotel renovation project. Trips can be taken into the national park, in boats or kayaks with a guide, through mangroves to the caves where there are pictographs.

East to Punta Cana listings

For hotel and restaurant price codes and other relevant information, see pages 10-13.

🛌 Where to stay

Boca Chica *p86*

Within easy reach of the capital and the airport visitors tend to stay for short breaks, sometimes only a night. The cheapest guesthouses are away from the beach up by the autopista, but for US$50-60 you can find a decent room closer to the sea. It is worth checking a hotel's policy regarding visitors, as prostitutes can be a nuisance. Do not leave valuables in your room. Even a locked safe can be burgled.

$$$ Hotel Zapata, Abraham Núñez 27, T8095234777, www.hotelzapata.com. Small hotel right on the beach, gated and secure. Simple but very clean rooms and suites, nothing fancy but adequate for most people's needs, those with balcony and sea view are best considering you are paying for the location. Friendly staff, good food.

$$$-$$ Calypso Beach Hotel, Caracol esq 20 de Diciembre, T809-523 4666. Not on beach, but close, some of the 40 rooms overlook the small pool, well kept, a/c, TV, pleasant, lots of plants, small bar, restaurant, buffet breakfast included.

$$$-$$ Garant, Sánchez 9, T809-523 5544, www.hotelgarant.com. Largest rooms are called suites, these and rooms on upper floor have a/c, downstairs economy rooms just have fan. You get a clean room, bed, TV, bathroom and fridge at a reasonable rate, cash only, small pool, restaurant, secure, locked gates, short walk to beach. Monthly rates available.

$$$-$$ Neptuno's Refugio, Duarte 17, T809-523 9934, neptunosrefugio@hotmail.com. Rooms, suites and apartments in 2 buildings on the seafront, one with sea view the other with pool view. Comfortable, simply furnished, quiet a/c, good breakfast, excellent service. Choose a room away from

the Hamaca Resort next door as nightlife there goes on until 0500 at weekends.

$$-$ El Tronco, Rogelio Alvarez 15, T809-523 6188, www.hotel-el-tronco.com. Rooms with fan, studios with a/c and fridge, apartments with kitchenette, small pool, security guard, 5-min walk to beach, Dutch-owned, Austrian-managed, lots of languages spoken. Can arrange airport transfers, diving and other excursions. Also owns Piano Plaza disco in town.

La Romana *p87*

$$$$ Casa de Campo, 10 km to the east of La Romana, T809-523 3333, www.casadecampo.com.do. The leading resort in the country, secure, private, popular with celebrities and the wealthy. Hotel, villas, bars, restaurants and country club. Lots of different packages for families, golf, tennis, etc.

Bayahibe *p88*

There are many all-inclusive hotels along the coast, on the edge of the village but mostly east along Playa Dominicus. It is more fun to stay in the village, particularly if you are a diver, as the dive shops are here and there are local bars and restaurants as well as more international options. Cabañas for rent, for around US$20-30, ask around, don't expect hot water.

$$$-$$ Cabana Elke, Playa Dominicus, T809-689 8249, www.viwi.it. Behind Wyndham Dominicus Beach, 3 km east of original village, with access to their grounds on purchase of a US$45-85 day pass (depending on time of year). Standard rooms look on to the road, small bathroom, can be joined to make an apartment. Apartments looking onto garden and pool have a large living area with sofa bed, kitchenette, shower room downstairs and loft bedroom upstairs. All have screened porches with chairs. Restaurant and bar. Discounts in low season.

$$$-$$ El Edén, Av Laguna 10, T809-833 0856. Pleasant small hotel in nice gardens with pool in walking distance of Playa Dominicus. Simple rooms have fan, a/c, hot water.

$$$-$$ Hotel Bayahibe, Calle Principal, T809-833 0159, www.hotelbayahibe.net. Best in village but it's often full, TV, fridge, reasonable showers, a/c or fan, balcony, 50 m to the water and dive boats. Breakfast is at their separate restaurant on the waterfront. Several restaurants in walking distance, as is public beach and dive shop.

$$ Villa Baya Aparta-Hotel, Calle El Tamarindo, T809-833 0408, www.hotel villabaya.com. Attractive development of rooms and studios with kitchenettes, those on upper floors have balconies, spacious bathrooms with hot water, firm beds, locked gate for security. Convenient for local supermarket with ATM and *colmado* attached for evening drinking. Take earplugs if cockerels bother you.

$ Cabañas Trip Town, Juan Brito, T809-224 5043. Simple rooms with fan or rather noisy a/c, fridge, cleaned daily, hot water, towels and soap provided. Locally owned, only Spanish spoken.

Bávaro *p90*

$$ Bávaro Hostel, Los Corales, Playa El Cortecito, T809-931 6767, www.bavaro hostel.com. For those who don't want to stay in an all-inclusive there are a few places in this area, within easy reach of beach, restaurants, shops, nightlife and bus station. Some of them are pretty seedy, but this hostel is new, clean, well equipped and friendly, with a strict 'no guest' policy and in a safe, well lit area. Rooms and dorms all with shared bathroom and kitchen.

Sabana de la Mar *p91*

$$$-$$ Ecolodge Paraíso Caño Hondo, Sabana de la Mar, T809-686 0278, www. paraisocanohondo.com. Tucked into the hillside, the varied rooms are simple with rustic decor, but comfortable, with fan and hot water. A river runs down the hill

channelled into waterfalls and 12 pools where you can bathe. Guides are available for walking tours or kayaking in the national park, also whale watching in season and other excursions such as rock climbing, horse riding, ziplining and birdwatching. Slow service in the restaurant.

🍴 Restaurants

Boca Chica *p86*

There are beach bars and stalls (*fritureras*) all along the beach selling fried fish, *yaniqueques*, sausages, and other local specialities as well as cold beer and soft drinks.

$$$ Boca Marina, Prolongación Duarte 12A, 1 block east of the Hamaca, T809-688 6810, www.bocamarina.com.do. Sun-Thu 1000-2400, Fri-Sat 1000-0100. Built over the water with a pier full of tables and comfy sofas, old colonial style furniture, lamps made of shells hanging from the palm thatched roof. Nice place to spend a day on the beach listening to good music and having a variety of food, good seafood, also great for sunset watching or a romantic dinner. Reservations strongly recommended, particularly at weekends and holiday times.

$$$ Neptunes Club, east of Hamaca, T809-523 4703. Built over water, with pier, good fish watching, swimming rafts, extensive menu including seafood, bar in replica of the *Santa María*. A good place to spend the day, swimming, eating and drinking, with basic showers to clean up afterwards.

La Romana *p87*

$$$-$ Shish Kabab, Castillo Márquez 32, T809-556 2737, jgiha@hotmail.com. The menu includes Arab dishes as well as Dominican and more international fare, but what most Dominicans come here for are the *quipes* and *empanadas de yuca*, sold in bags for taking home or to eat in. The cracked wheat *quipes* are hot, crispy and tasty, so order plenty. Service isn't great so you have to be proactive in getting the waiters' attention, like the locals.

Bayahibe *p88*

$$$ Chikyblu, on the waterfront, T809-833 0514, pino57sp@inwind.it. This Italian bar and restaurant has great pizza and pasta and real Italian food, while it also serves sushi. A pretty spot with a good view, it gets very busy at night, with a devoted Italian clientele.

Bávaro *p90*

$$$ Balicana, Villa Los Corales, Los Corales, T829-898 4479. Pleasant poolside restaurant with candlelit tables and lounge area, serving Thai and Malaysian food using local ingredients. Also good juices, such as mango when in season, and alcoholic drinks, do try the passion fruit margarita. Credit cards accepted.

$$$ Capitán Cook, Playa El Cortecito, T809-552 1061. An independent restaurant on the beach with plenty of shade, or a balcony upstairs. Specialities include fresh lobster, shrimp and fish caught locally, which you can see before you choose. Steak and a *parrillada* are also available for those who don't eat fish. A vibrant atmosphere.

$$-$ Chickeeta Bonita's, Av Alemania, Plaza Arenal Caribe, Los Corales. 0800-2200. Good place for breakfast, lunch, snacks, coffee and 18 flavours of ice cream. Canadian-run with multilingual, helpful staff. Book exchange.

What to do

Boca Chica *p86*
Diving
Caribbean Divers, Duarte 44, T809-854 3483, www.caribbeandivers.de. German-run with multilingual staff offering a full range of courses and qualifications. Local dive sites include wrecks and reefs. Staff are experienced and knowledgeable as well as helpful and caring with beginners or nervous divers.

Bayahibe *p88*
Diving
The all-inclusive resorts have their own dive operations.
Scubafun, Calle Principal 28, T809-833 0003, www.scubafun.info. An independent dive shop, clients range from **Casa de Campo** guests to backpackers, beginners to experienced divers. They are very flexible and will do almost anything on request. 2-tank dives with a beach stop cost US$80, a trip to Saona, Catalina or Catalinita, including national park fees, drinks and snacks, costs an additional US$55-79. Day trip to Saona Island costs US$69.

Transport

Boca Chica *p86*
Bus
Guagua from Santo Domingo US$2 from either Parque Enriquillo or Parque Independencia, or the corner of San Martín and Av París but not after dark. **Boca Chica Express**, US$2, 30-40 mins, stops running around 2100.

Car
If driving from the capital, look carefully for signposts to whichever part of Boca Chica you wish to go. Numerous parking attendants will offer spots along the beach.

Taxi
Santo Domingo-Boca Chica US$30-40 (can be only US$20 from Boca Chica to Santo Domingo), US$20 from the airport.

La Romana *p87*
Air
La Romana International Airport (LRM), just beside the Autopista del Coral, east of La Romana, receives **American Airlines**, **WestJet**, **JetBlue** and **Air Canada** from North America, **Condor** and **Air Berlin** from Germany.

Altos de Chavón *p88*
Bus and taxi
Free bus every 15 mins from **Casa de Campo**. Taxi from La Romana, US$20-25. Most people arrive on tour buses or hired car.

Bayahibe *p88*
Bus and taxi
A *guagua* La Romana-Bayahibe is US$1.50 to the *colmado* in the village. A taxi from La Romana costs about US$30-40.

Punta Cana *p90*
Air
Flights vary according to season. Punta Cana (PUJ) receives more passengers than any other airport in the country.

From North America American Airlines, US Airways, Air Canada, JetBlue, Air Transat.

From Europe Condor, Air Europa, Air France, British Airways, Thompson Flights, Thomas Cook. For a full list of airlines, see www.puntacanainternationalairport.com/flight-info/airlines.

Southwest

The far southwest of the Republic is a dry zone with typical dry-forest vegetation. It also contains some of the country's most spectacular coastline and several national parks. It is a mountainous area with great views and scary roads and the closer you get to the Haitian border the poorer and more deforested the country becomes. This was the major cause of the devastation after heavy rains in 2004. It may never be known how many thousands of people lost their lives in mud slides at Jimaní and across the border in Haiti, where there were no trees to hold the soil in place. Tourism is not big business here yet, although there are some fascinating places to visit, such as Lago Enriquillo, a saltwater lake below sea level and three times saltier than the sea, or the mines for larimar, a pale blue semi-precious stone used in jewellery. The towns and villages are unremarkable and unpretentious but give a fascinating insight into rural and provincial life in the Republic.

San Cristóbal and around → *For listings, see pages 103-105.*

San Cristóbal

The birthplace of the dictator Rafael Leonidas Trujillo, San Cristóbal is 25 km west of Santo Domingo. Most of the sites of interest are related to his involvement with the town. He was on his way to San Cristóbal to visit a mistress when he was gunned down. Two roads lead west out of Santo Domingo: 6 de Noviembre bypasses the port of Haina and San Cristóbal, while 9 de Mayo is the coastal road, named after the day Trujillo was assassinated on the road. Both of Trujillo's homes are now in ruins but can be visited. The **Casa de Caoba** was looted and stripped bare after the dictator's death, but still gives an idea of the building's former opulence, when it was lined with mahogany. Take the turning off the dual carriageway from Santo Domingo signed to La Toma de San Cristóbal, bypassing the city. Turn right after the purple PLD office and then stop just after the water tank on your left. The 1-km road up to the house is on your left, but a sturdy 4WD is required – it is better to walk. A caretaker will let you in and show you around for a tip. The **Palacio del Cerro** was another luxury residence on top of a hill with a tremendous view. The Palacio is run down, although there are more decorative features than at the Casa de Caoba, including a grand marble staircase, a gold and silver mosaic-tiled bathroom and a heliport on the roof. From the Parque Central follow the Baní road, Avenida Luperón, and turn left at the Isla petrol station. The house is guarded by the military, for a tip someone will show you around.

El Pomier

The caves at El Pomier protected by the **Reserva Antropológica de las Cuevas de Borbón**, are some 15 km north out of town (pick-up truck from market on Juanto María and Fco Peynado leave when full, US$0.25, or motoconcho US$1.25) on the road to La Toma de San Cristóbal. From Santo Domingo take the 6 de Noviembre highway to La Toma crossroads, turn right and drive to the broken bridge over the Arroyo Carvajal, turn left and go 2 km until you get to the limestone factory, from where you follow a dirt road to the main office at the reserve. The caves are of enormous archaeological value, considered to be as important for the Caribbean Basin as Egypt's pyramids are for the Middle East. The reserve comprises over 6000 pictographs and some 500 petroglyphs, the largest collection in the Caribbean, primarily by the Taíno, but also by the Carib and the Igneri. Espeleogrupo de Santo Domingo is working to protect the caves and their drawings, but face considerable opposition from mining companies in the area. The caves are not officially open to tourists and have been unlit since the electric cables were stolen, so strong flashlights and good boots are necessary and you should go in with a guide. Contact Domingo Abreu Collado, President of the **Espeleogrupo de Santo Domingo** ① T809-383 4078, *espeleo99@yahoo.com*.

Palenque, Nigua and Najayo

South of San Cristóbal, the beaches at Palenque, Nigua and Najayo (*públicos* leave regularly from San Cristóbal's Parque Central) are mostly of grey sand. On a hill overlooking Najayo beach are the ruins of Trujillo's beach house. These beaches are popular as excursions from Santo Domingo and at weekends and holidays can be packed. Lots of beach bars serve finger-licking fried fish and local food, washed down with ice cold beer. The music can be overbearing at times with sound systems competing against each other on the beach. At Palenque the dark sand beach is deserted at the far end and you don't have to walk far to get away from the crowds. Good swimming at Palenque, rougher at Najayo but there is an artificial wave breaker.

Baní and Las Salinas → *For listings, see pages 103-105.*

Baní

From San Cristóbal the road runs west through sugar cane country to Baní, known for its mangos, sweet corn and desserts, such as *majarete*, which looks like a cheesecake, and *chen chen*, maize cooked like rice. The Banilejo mango, small, pink and very sweet, is in season in April-July. Look out for roadside stops where you can sample many sweet things. Baní is the birthplace of Máximo Gómez, the 19th-century fighter for the liberation of Cuba. The **Casa de Máximo Gómez** ① *Av Máximo Gómez, daily 0800-1200, free*, is a museum with a mural in his memory, set in a shady plaza within walking distance of the main Parque Duarte, the centre of the town and a pleasant spot. The small house is at the back of a pretty park marked by a bust of the hero at the entrance and flags flying at either side. There is a great deal on his biography, as well as general history of the period, photos and old documents, but no personal belongings. The lady guardian speaks some English.

Las Salinas and around

Of the two roads west out of Baní, take the one to Las Calderas naval base for Las Salinas. There is no problem in going through the base (photography is not allowed); after it, turn left for 3 km to the fishing village of Las Salinas, passing the sand dunes of the **Bahía de**

Calderas, now a national monument and an inlet on the Bahía de Ocoa, shallow, with some mangroves and good windsurfing and fishing. The dunes, the largest in the Caribbean, can be reached from the road, but there are no facilities and little shade. The views are spectacular, however, as are the biting insects, so cover yourself in repellent before venturing onto the sand. The salt flats at Las Salinas are no longer in commercial operation, but if you drive past them to the end of the road you get to Punta Salinas, where there is a thatched restaurant and disco open at weekends and a tourist police office on the beach.

A pleasant detour off the main road takes you to **Palmar de Ocoa**, a fishing village on the eastern side of the Bahía de Ocoa, in what has become a popular area for weekenders 99 km from the capital. There are lots of smart holiday homes along the coast but the village remains quiet with rows of fishing boats pulled up on the grey sand and pebble shore. The setting is beautiful, looking across the bay to the mountains inland.

The main road west carries on from Baní through Azua to Barahona. The landscape is at first extremely dry, with los scrub and cactus on the hillsides and few settlements. **Azua** is an isolated town in one of the hottest and most unwelcoming parts of the Republic, although it has a long and distinguished history, having been founded in 1504.

Barahona and around → *For listings, see pages 103-105.*

Barahona

Barahona is a comparatively young town, founded in 1802 by the Haitian leader, Toussaint Louverture, when he was briefly in control of the whole of Hispaniola. Its economy initially rested on the export to Europe of precious woods, for example mahogany. In the 20th century the sugar industry took over. The main attractions of this rather run-down grid-system town revolve around the seafront **Malecón**, where most hotels and restaurants are to be found. There is an attractive park with an old train, a sports area and playground. The **Parque Central**, five blocks up, is the commercial hub of the town. It is a noisy town, the traffic is heavy and there are lots of *motos*. The small, public beach at Barahona frequently has stinging jelly fish. It is also filthy, as is the sea, and theft is common. The best beach near town is called **El Cayo** and is reached by passing the sugar mill and surrounding slums and doubling back on to the sandy peninsula with palms (visible from the **Brisas del Caribe** restaurant).

Laguna Rincón/Cabral

Northwest of Barahona is the Laguna Rincón/Cabral, the largest freshwater lake in the country, a Wildlife Refuge and a Ramsar wetland site of international importance since 2011. Home to both endemic and migratory birds, many water plants and endemic fish, there are also many reptiles, snakes, lizards and iguanas. Boat tours are available, best taken October-March for the variety of wildlife.

Beaches south of Barahona

Those with a car can visit remote beaches from Barahona (public transport is limited to *públicos*). The coast road south of Barahona runs through some of the most beautiful scenery in the Republic, mountains on one side, the sea on the other, leading to Pedernales on the Haitian border (146 km). All along the southern coast are many white-sand beaches with some of the best snorkelling in the Republic. The first place is the pebble beach of **El Quemaito**, where the river comes out across the beach, the cold freshwater mixing with the warm sea; offshore is a reef.

Las Filipinas

At the end of the village of Las Filipinas, about 14 km from Barahona, turn right on to a dirt road. Inland about 15 km into the hills along a very poor track (4WD essential, especially after rain, ask directions at the nearby *colmado*) are the open-cast mines where the semi-precious mineral, larimar, is dug. Larimar is mined only in the Dominican Republic and is mostly used for jewellery. Miners or local boys will sell you fragments of stone, usually in jars of water to enhance the colour, for US$5-10, depending on size and colour. When dry, larimar is a paler blue.

San Rafael Natural Springs

Back on the main road, you pass through **Baoruco** (see Where to stay) and **La Ciénaga** (small stony beaches and rough tides). The road comes right down to the sea before San Rafael natural springs (about 40 minutes from Barahona) where a river runs out onto a stony beach. The forest grows to the edge of the beach. Where the road crosses the river is a *pensión* with a free cold water swimming hole, *balneario*, behind it (the swimming hole is safer than the sea as enormous waves surge onto the beach). At weekends it gets very crowded. There are normally a number of stalls selling drinks and fried fish. It is also possible to climb up the mountain alongside the river, which has small waterfalls and pools.

South to Oviedo → *For listings, see pages 103-105.*

At El Paraíso, a medium-sized town 31 km from Barahona, are a popular beach, Texaco station and many *colmados*, *comedores* and bars. The river here, Río Nizaíto, flows pale blue from the larimar sediment, forming a large semi-circle of milky blue where it runs out into the sea, particularly impressive after rain. Inland from here, 20 minutes up a rough track, is the delightful **Rancho Platón** (see Where to stay, below), from where you can go hiking in sub-tropical humid forest, horse riding or tubing on the river. Half an hour further up into the cloud forest is **El Cachote**, at 1000 m, a centre for community tourism where there is a rustic lodge with dormitory accommodation used for groups. The area is a rural idyll, with good hiking and great birdwatching. Many of the island's endemic bird species can be found here. Botanists will also be rewarded with the huge variety of plant life in the cloud forest, which forms the eastern part of the **Parque Nacional Sierra de Bahoruco**. This one of the country's wildest regions, densely covered in pine forests and sub-tropical rainforest, although parts have been illegally cleared and logged. This remote district was where the legendary Taíno chieftan **Enriquillo** staged his resistance to the Spanish conquistadores from 1519 to 1533, setting up an independent community in the mountains and holding the Spanish at bay for almost 15 years. Near the village of **Aguacate**, where there is a military outpost, the **Loma del Toro** stands at an altitude of 2367 m in an area where high and humid conditions encourage a wide range of orchids (more than 150 varieties) and an unusual diversity of trees. The park is also home to a rish array of birds, including Hispaniolan parakeets, Hispaniolan trogons and La Selle's thrush.

At **Los Patos** another river flows into the sea to form a cool bathing place; a great place to spend the day at a weekend to watch Dominicans at play, with excellent swimming and lots of family groups. There are several *comedores* serving fresh fish and other seafood. **La Chorrea** is a man-made pool from a natural spring about five minutes' drive up a dirt road on the right-hand side. There are cool, freshwater lagoons behind several of the other beaches on this stretch of coast. **Laguna Limón** is a flamingo reserve. A startling sight on your right as you drive along the main road is the presence of an enormous wind farm, one of the Republic's first forays into alternative energy sources, in stark contrast to the poor villages in the area.

Enriquillo, 54 km south of Barahona, is the last place for fuel until Pedernales, 80 km away, but no unleaded is available. After Enriquillo the road turns inland up to Oviedo and then skirts the Parque Nacional Jaragua as it runs a further 60 km to Pedernales. **Oviedo**, with the atmosphere of a desert settlement, has no hotels or decent restaurants and is one of the hottest places in the country.

Parque Nacional Jaragua → *For listings, see pages 103-105.*

ⓘ *Ministry of the Environment office just outside Oviedo in Cajuil; daily 0830-1630, entry US$2.50; a boat tour on Laguna Oviedo costs around US$75, for up to 5 visitors. For information on the flora and fauna of the area as well as threats to the environment, particularly deforestation for agriculture, see www.grupojaragua.org.do.*

Parque Nacional Jaragua is the largest of the Dominican Republic's national parks and part of the UNESCO Biosphere Reserve Jaragua-Bahoruco-Enriquillo formed in 2002. This area of subtropical dry forest and inhospitable prickly scrub also contains a marine zone, in which lie the uninhabited islands of **Beata** and **Alto Velo**. The vegetation is largely cactus and other desert plants, but there are also mahogany, frangipani and extensive mangroves. Of particular interest is the **Laguna Oviedo** at the eastern end of the park, which is easily accessible from Oviedo. Here there are the country's largest population of flamingos as well as herons, terns, spoonbills and frigate birds. Animals include the Ricord iguana, the rhinoceros iguana and several species of bat. The lagoon is reached via the national park office just outside Oviedo where an entrance permit must be bought. There is a viewing tower for a great view over the lake. Boat trips are highly recommended to see birds and iguanas and also a couple of Taíno cave sites with pictograms as well as a beach on the other side.

Also in the national park is **Bahía de las Aguilas**, one of the most pristine and virginal beaches in the country. The area is under threat of development for tourism, so you are recommended to visit before the hotels move in. From Oviedo, continue on Route 44 towards Pedernales. In parts, this is a dead straight road, but beware of hazards such as cows and the inevitable demise of hundreds of butterflies. At the intersection of Cabo Rojo, head south towards the cement plant. The beach at Cabo Rojo has lovely clear water and white sand, while the soil behind the beach is red with iron, but it is marred by the Cementos Andinos dock and cement plant. Local and Haitian fishermen come in here and it is possible to buy fish from them early in the morning and take it to the beach to barbecue it. From here take the unpaved road for 5 km along the coast heading east to the small fishing community called **La Cueva** on the very edge of the national park. You pay your Park US$2.50 entry fee here. There are brightly painted fishermen's huts which have been moved out of the park, some of which are rented out to tourists. There is a restaurant with good, clean bathrooms and camping is possible with your own tent. From here boat passage may be negotiated for around US$80 (there and back, arrange a collection time) for up to 10 people to a make the 10-minute journey round the cliffs of the headland to the sandy-white and desolate shores of Bahía de las Aguilas. Alternatively you can walk, a very hot hike of 30-45 minutes requiring lots of water, while some locals with 4WD or quad bikes drive over the hill on a very poor track. Definitely bring water, sunscreen, and appropriate attire for the weather as there are absolutely no services available in the area. The only shade is under the scrubby trees behind the beach. You can walk all around the 4.4-km bay and not see a soul, although at weekends there may be some other people.

Birth of a colony, death of a people

Columbus visited the north coast of Hispaniola, modern Haiti, on his first visit to the West Indies, leaving a few men there to make a settlement before he moved on to Cuba. He traded with the native Taínos for trinkets, which were to seal the Indians' fate when shown to the Spanish monarchs. A second voyage was ordered immediately. Columbus tried again to establish settlements, his first having been wiped out. His undisciplined men were soon at war with the native Taínos, who were hunted, taxed and enslaved. Hundreds were shipped to Spain, where they died. When Columbus had to return to Spain he left his brother, Bartolomé, in charge of the fever-ridden, starving colony. The latter sensibly moved the settlement to the healthier south coast and founded Santo Domingo, which became the capital of the Spanish Indies. The native inhabitants were gradually eliminated by European diseases, murder, suicide and slavery, while their crops were destroyed by newly introduced herds of cattle and pigs. Development was hindered by the labour shortage and the island became merely a base from which to provision further exploration, being a source of bacon, dried beef and cassava. Even the alluvial gold dwindled and could not compete with discoveries on the mainland. The population of some 400,000 Taínos in 1492 fell to about 60,000 by 1508. In 1512 the Indians were declared free subjects of Spain, and missionary zeal ensured their conversion to Christianity. A further 40,000 were brought from the Turks and Caicos, the Bahamas and Venezuela, but by 1525 the Indian population had practically disappeared. Sugar was introduced at the beginning of the 16th century and the need for labour soon brought African slaves.

Far west → For listings, see pages 103-105.

Pedernales

Pedernales is the most westerly town of the Republic, on the Haitian border. This is a major crossing point for migrant Haitian workers who come over to work in the sugar cane plantations and in construction. There is no road link, but there is a footbridge across the river that divides the countries. Every Monday and Friday there is an informal market in the no man's land at the border crossing, where Haitians sell cheap counterfeit clothing brands, smuggled spirits and a vast array of plastic kitchenware. At the military stop on the Dominican side of the border you can find a Haitian guide, who will accompany you into Haiti, show you around the extremely poor fishing village on the other side of the bridge and bring you back for a tip of about US$10-15. Pedernales is the closest place to stay if you want to visit Bahía de las Aguilas.

Parque Nacional Isla Cabritos

ⓘ *Purchase a Dirección Nacional de Parques (DNP) permit (US$2.50) at the ranger station east of La Descubierta (0700-1500) to visit the island; only groups with a guide are permitted to go there. The 30-min boat trip to the island is offered by various local boatmen, who are recommended by the DNP staff.*

Near the Haitian border is the **Lago Enriquillo**, whose waters, below sea level, are three times saltier than the sea. Once linked to the bay of Port-au-Prince and the Bahía de Neiba, the lake was cut off from the sea by tectonic movements some million years ago and the surrounding beaches and the islands are rich in ancient seashells and coral fragments. Wildlife includes about 500 American crocodiles and iguanas. The island of Isla Cabritos, together with the lake and surrounding shoreline, make up the Parque Nacional Isla Cabritos. Isla Cabritos is a flat expanse of parched sand, with cactus and other desert vegetation. It is extremely hot and oppressive around midday (temperatures have been known to rise to 50°C) and visitors are recommended to arrive as early as possible and to take water and precautions against sunburn. This barren island is home to the rhinoceros iguana and the Ricord iguana, both of which have become quite tame, even aggressive, and approach boat parties in search of treats. To visit the lake it is best to have your own transport because public transport can not be guaranteed. Note that there is a filling station in Duvergé but no fuel elsewhere in this area.

Lago Enriquillo used to measure 200 sq km in 2004, but then it started to grow. As the salty waters rose, they flooded farmland and roads, killing trees and impoverishing farmers. The flamingos left when there were no beaches for them to wade from. Only the crocodiles have benefited, finding it easier to steal goats and chickens from their shrinking pasture. The landing stage for boat trips from the DNP office is under water. At the end of 2012, the lake was estimated at 350 sq km and two small islands, Barbarita and La Islita had completely disappeared. Studies are underway and there are many theories, but no one has yet proved why the water is still rising. Some roads have been reinforced and others relocated uphill, but there is no guarantee that they won't get flooded again. In 2013 a new housing project, Pueblo Verde, was started to provide 537 homes for families displaced by the flooding. Pressure to provide replacement land for farmers brought conflict with conservationists when the Minister of the Environment approved the clearing of over 100 ha of the Charco Azul Biological Reserve, part of the UNESCO Biosphere Reserve. The Reserve is the habitat for the Ricord iguana, found only in the Dominican Republic and known for its blood-red eyes, and other endemic species such as the Hispaniolan racer snake (*Haitiophis anomalus*), a tree cactus (*Dendrocereus undulosus*) and the endangered solenodon (see page 75).

East of the DNP station for Lago Enriquillo is **Las Caritas**, said to have been a holy site for the Taínos and a possible hiding place for Enriquillo. A series of indistinct faces have been carved in the coral stone up on the hillside. Handrails and some rough steps lead steeply up to the carvings, from where you get a panoramic view over Lake Enriquillo, particularly beautiful at sunset.

La Descubierta is a pleasant and quiet town. The centre of most activity is at the public *balneario* of **Las Barías**, a pretty spot and cool under the trees. The community area serves local dishes, accompanied by 1.5-litre bottles of hot sauce.

Jimaní

Jimaní, at the western end of the lake, is a spread-out town of single-storey housing which swelters in temperatures of up to 50°C, about 2 km from the Haitian border. The space in between is a no man's land of rocky terrain crossed by an extremely hot road, which has a constant coming and going of *guaguas* and *motoconchos*. Jimaní is an authorized crossing point for foreigners in general (as is Dajabón) and it is possible to leave the Dominican Republic here and cross into Haiti. Customs officers in Jimaní are not above taking items from your luggage. The immigration office closes at 1800 (or before). There is a semi-permanent market in the no man's land, in which Haitian merchants sell food, household items, Barbancourt rum and perfumes. However, because of flooding of Etang Soumâtre in Haiti as with Lake Enriquillo, the area formerly used on the Haitian side of the border is now under water and everything is squeezed into a small patch on the Dominican side. Even here, warehouses are already flooded and useless, while the road is partially under water despite having been raised and reinforced. Reclamation efforts appear futile.

Southwest listings

For hotel and restaurant price codes and other relevant information, see pages 10-13.

🛏 Where to stay

Baní and Las Salinas *p97*
$$$ Salinas, Las Salinas, Puerto Hermoso 7, Baní, T809-866 8141, hotel_salinas@hotmail.com. Price per person. Hotel and restaurant run by Jorge Domenech and his family. All-inclusive rates available, which include any drinks and meals are à la carte. Very good food. Rooms and suites on the waterfront with lovely views across the bay, especially from the upper floors (no elevator). Marble luxury with rustic elegance, but you can still find holes in the walls, exposed wiring and doors falling off kitchen units. Great for windsurfers and kiteboarders (bring your own equipment) and fishermen, many guests arrive in their own boat and tie up at the jetty (where there is also a helipad), diving can be arranged with local boatmen (bring your own gear).

Palmar de Ocoa *p98*
$$$ Ibiza, Wiche García Zaleta, Playa Chiquita, T809-866 8141, hotelibizapalmar@hotmail.com. Also owned by Jorge Domenech, outside the village, remote, nothing in walking distance and on a stony beach, but quiet with lovely view of the bay. 12 rooms with whitewashed furniture, new and of a good standard.

Barahona *p98*
$$$$ Casa Bonita, Ctra de la Costa Km 16, Baoruco, T809-476 5059, www.casabonitadr.com. One of the Small Luxury Hotels of the World. One of the loveliest places to stay in the country, on a hillside overlooking coast, wonderful views of the sierra and the sea. Rooms and suites all have view, stylish, tropical elegance in rustic surroundings, peaceful, wonderful food, all locally sourced. Delightful spa with Taíno-influenced treatments, pool and even a zipline through the forest.
$$$$ Rancho Platón, T829-886 1836, www.ranchoplaton.com. A very special place high up in the hills beside the larimar-blue Río Nizao. 4WD is essential to get there as the track is rough, but the hotel will collect you from Paraíso if necessary, leaving your car at their fuel station on the Malecón. Lovely, timber rooms, but the 2 best are in a tree house, fabulous being high up, hammocks and deck for relaxing and view, magical at sunset. Lots of activities, tubing on the river, hiking, waterslide, spa treatments. Horses are unfortunately skinny, with sores, so check your animal before riding.
$$$$-$$$ Piratas del Caribe, Arzobispo Nouel 1, Paraíso Playa, T809-243 1140, www.hotelpiratasdelcaribe.com. Small hotel on the beach, family-run, huge and attractive rooms, each with balcony/terrace, restaurant, room service at no extra cost, excellent food, bottled water daily in bathroom, TV, a/c, fan, massages, pool, efficient and friendly service.
$$$ La Saladilla Beach Club, La Saladilla, 2 km from Barahona, T809-667 8939. Small, family-run, modern hotel with pool above a little beach with rocks and some good snorkelling. All meals available, good food, particularly the fresh fish and seafood. Spacious rooms, suites and apartment with kitchenette, well furnished, friendly and helpful service. Excursions can be arranged.
$$$-$ Hotel Quemaíto, Juan Esteban Km 10, Ctra Paraíso about 500 m down a dirt road on the left-hand side leaving Barahona, T809-649 7631, www.hotelelquemaito.com. The hotel sits on a cliff about 30 m above

the water and has stunning views of a small inlet below and sprawling green lawns. Some rooms have small terraces. One dorm room with bunk beds and separate shower. Many languages spoken. German chef prepares local and international dishes using fruit and vegetables from organic hotel farm in the mountains.

$$ Caribe, Av Enriquillo, T809-524 4111. All rooms have private bath, TV, fan, a/c, breakfast included. Adequate for a night or two but basic and showing its age.

$$ Loro Tuerto, Luis E Delmonte 33, T809-524 6600, www.lorotuerto.com. On the main road, short walk to the market and the bus station opposite, a traditional wooden house in the old style, with a block of rooms behind. Upstairs rooms are the best, all with a/c, breakfast, own generator. Service affable but slow.

Pedernales *p101*

$$ Hostal Doña Chava, PN Hugson (Calle 2) 5, Barrio Alcoa, T809-524 0332, hostalchava@hotmail.com. On the edge of town but in walking distance of supermarket, restaurants and bars. Simple, small rooms but OK for the price, Staff will help you find transport to local sights.

$$ Villas del Mar, Cacique Enriquillo 2, Barrio Miramar, T809-524 0448, ferreras_victor@yahoo.es. Reasonable rooms with a/c, fan, TV, Wi-Fi, pool, access to stony beach where you can swim, or you can walk along to a better spot. Restaurant.

🍴 Restaurants

Barahona *p98*

There are lots of places to eat along the waterfront, which get lively at night, particularly at weekends when the bars are busy and noisy with blaring music. Outside town, the hotels listed above have the best food, although small *comedores* and weekend barbeques can be found at river bathing spots for a good fish fry.

$$$ Brisas del Caribe, Av Enriquillo, at northern end of Malecón, T809-524 2794. 0900-2300. Excellent seafood restaurant, popular at lunchtime, reasonable prices, pleasant setting.

Parque Nacional Jaragua *p100*

$$$ Rancho Típico, Cueva de las Aguilas, T809-753 8058, cuevadelasaguilas@hotmail.com. Restaurant and bar at the very edge of the national park, from where you can get a boat around the cliffs to the beach. Snorkelling trips and boats to Isla Beata also arranged. Good seafood and local dishes. The catch of the day is usually a very large fish, served in a variety of ways, great with *tostones* and a cold beer for lunch.

⚪ What to do

San Cristóbal *p96*
Tour operators

Domingo Abreu, T809-682 1577, domingoespele87@hotmail.com. Runs tours from Santo Domingo to El Pomier caves, giving an excellent guided tour of the main chambers and less frequently visited ones too, where you can see a huge quantity of rock art and lots of bats. It involves a lot of scrambling and rappelling, so go appropriately dressed with good footwear.

Barahona *p98*
Tour operators

Ecotour Barahona, Calle Enriquillo, Edif 7, 2nd floor, Paraíso de Barahona, or Padre Billini 405, Zona Colonial, Santo Domingo, T809-243 1190, www.ecotourbarahona.com. A wide variety of nature and adventure tours to the area's national parks, from day trips to multi-day packages with expert guides.

Julio Féliz, T809-524 6570. Is an English-speaking local guide who specializes in ecotourism and birdwatching, fees negotiable.

⊖ Transport

Barahona *p98*
Air
The international María Montéz Airport, opened in 1996 but is little used so far.

Bus
Journey time from **Santo Domingo** is 3 hrs. Caribe Tours runs 4 buses a day, US$6.75.

Contents

Footnotes

Basic Spanish for travellers

Learning Spanish is a useful part of the preparation for a trip to Latin America and no volumes of dictionaries, phrase books or word lists will provide the same enjoyment as being able to communicate directly with the people of the country you are visiting. It is a good idea to make an effort to grasp the basics before you go. As you travel you will pick up more of the language and the more you know, the more you will benefit from your stay.

General pronunciation

Whether you have been taught the 'Castilian' pronunciation (*z* and *c* followed by *i* or *e* are pronounced as the *th* in think) or the 'American' pronunciation (they are pronounced as *s*), you will encounter little difficulty in understanding either. Regional accents and usages vary, but the basic language is essentially the same everywhere.

Vowels

a	as in English *cat*
e	as in English *best*
i	as the ee in English *feet*
o	as in English *shop*
u	as the oo in English *food*
ai	as the i in English *ride*
ei	as ey in English *they*
oi	as oy in English *toy*

Consonants

Most consonants can be pronounced more or less as they are in English. The exceptions are:

g	before *e* or *i* is the same as *j*
h	is always silent (except in *ch* as in *chair*)
j	as the *ch* in Scottish *loch*
ll	as the *y* in *yellow*
ñ	as the *ni* in *onion*
rr	trilled much more than in English
x	depending on its location, pronounced *x*, *s*, *sh* or *j*

Spanish words and phrases

Greetings, courtesies

hello	*hola*	thank you (very much)	*(muchas) gracias*
good morning	*buenos días*	I don't speak Spanish	*no hablo español*
good afternoon/	*buenas tardes/*	do you speak English?	*¿habla inglés?*
evening/night	*noches*	I don't understand	*no comprendo*
goodbye	*adiós/chao*	please speak slowly	*hable despacio*
pleased to meet you	*mucho gusto*		*por favor*
how are you?	*¿cómo está?*	I am very sorry	*lo siento mucho/*
	¿cómo estás?		*disculpe*
I'm fine, thanks	*estoy muy bien,*	what do you want?	*¿qué quiere?*
	gracias		*¿qué quieres?*
I'm called...	*me llamo ...*	I want	*quiero*
what is your name?	*¿cómo se llama?*	I don't want it	*no lo quiero*
	¿cómo te llamas?	leave me alone	*déjeme en paz/*
yes/no	*sí/no*		*no me moleste*
please	*por favor*	good/bad	*bueno/malo*

Questions and requests

have you got a room for two people?	¿tiene una habitación para dos personas?
how do I get to_?	¿cómo llego a_?
how much does it cost?	¿cuánto cuesta? ¿cuánto es?
I'd like to make a long-distance phone call	quisiera hacer una llamada de larga distancia
is service included?	¿está incluido el servicio?
is tax included?	¿están incluidos los impuestos?
when does the bus leave (arrive)?	¿a qué hora sale (llega) el autobús?
when?	¿cuándo?
where is_?	¿dónde está_?
where can I buy tickets?	¿dónde puedo comprar boletos?
where is the nearest petrol station?	¿dónde está la gasolinera más cercana?
why?	¿por qué?

Basic words and phrases

bank	el banco	expensive	caro/a
bathroom/toilet	el baño	market	el mercado
bill	la factura/la cuenta	note/coin	el billete/la moneda
cash	el efectivo	police (policeman)	la policía (el policía)
cheap	barato/a	post office	el correo
credit card	la tarjeta de crédito	public telephone	el teléfono público
exchange house	la casa de cambio	supermarket	el supermercado
exchange rate	el tipo de cambio	ticket office	la taquilla

Getting around

aeroplane	el avión	insured person	el/la asegurado/a
airport	el aeropuerto	to insure yourself against	asegurarse contra
arrival/departure	la llegada/salida	luggage	el equipaje
avenue	la avenida	motorway, freeway	el autopista/
block	la cuadra		la carretera
border	la frontera	north, east	norte, este (oriente),
bus station	la terminal	south, west	sur, oeste (occidente)
	de autobuses	oil	el aceite
bus	el autobús/la guagua	to park	estacionarse
collective/	el colectivo	passport	el pasaporte
fixed-route taxi		petrol/gasoline	la gasolina
corner	la esquina	puncture	el pinchazo/
customs	la aduana		la ponchadura
first/second class	primera/segunda clase	street	la calle
left/right	izquierda/derecha	that way	por allí/por allá
ticket	el billete	this way	por aquí/por acá
empty/full	vacío/lleno	tyre	la llanta
highway, main road	la carretera	unleaded	sin plomo
immigration	la inmigración	to walk	caminar/andar
insurance	el seguro		

Index

Titles available ~~DATE DUE~~ ... range

Latin America	UK RRP	US RRP
Bahia & Salvador	£7.99	$11.95
Brazilian Amazon	£7.99	$11.95
Brazilian Pantanal	£6.99	$9.95
Buenos Aires & Pampas	£7.99	$11.95
Cartagena & Caribbean Coast	£7.99	$11.95
Costa Rica	£8.99	$12.95
Cuzco, La Paz & Lake Titicaca	£8.99	$12.95
El Salvador	£5.99	$8.95
Guadalajara & Pacific Coast	£6.99	$9.95
Guatemala	£8.99	$12.95
Guyana, Guyane & Suriname	£5.99	$8.95
Havana	£6.99	$9.95
Honduras	£7.99	$11.95
Nicaragua	£7.99	$11.95
Northeast Argentina & Uruguay	£8.99	$12.95
Paraguay	£5.99	$8.95
Quito & Galápagos Islands	£7.99	$11.95
Recife & Northeast Brazil	£7.99	$11.95
Rio de Janeiro	£8.99	$12.95
São Paulo	£5.99	$8.95
Uruguay	£6.99	$9.95
Venezuela	£8.99	$12.95
Yucatán Peninsula	£6.99	$9.95

Asia	UK RRP	US RRP
Angkor Wat	£5.99	$8.95
Bali & Lombok	£8.99	$12.95
Chennai & Tamil Nadu	£8.99	$12.95
Chiang Mai & Northern Thailand	£7.99	$11.95
Goa	£6.99	$9.95
Gulf of Thailand	£8.99	$12.95
Hanoi & Northern Vietnam	£8.99	$12.95
Ho Chi Minh City & Mekong Delta	£7.99	$11.95
Java	£7.99	$11.95
Kerala	£7.99	$11.95
Kolkata & West Bengal	£5.99	$8.95
Mumbai & Gujarat	£8.99	$12.95

Africa & Middle East	UK RRP	US RRP
Beirut	£6.99	$9.95
Cairo & Nile Delta	£8.99	$12.95
Damascus	£5.99	$8.95
Durban & KwaZulu Natal	£8.99	$12.95
Fès & Northern Morocco	£8.99	$12.95
Jerusalem	£8.99	$12.95
Johannesburg & Kruger National Park	£7.99	$11.95
Kenya's Beaches	£8.99	$12.95
Kilimanjaro & Northern Tanzania	£8.99	$12.95
Luxor to Aswan	£8.99	$12.95
Nairobi & Rift Valley	£7.99	$11.95
Red Sea & Sinai	£7.99	$11.95
Zanzibar & Pemba	£7.99	$11.95

Europe	UK RRP	US RRP
Bilbao & Basque Region	£6.99	$9.95
Brittany West Coast	£7.99	$11.95
Cádiz & Costa de la Luz	£6.99	$9.95
Granada & Sierra Nevada	£6.99	$9.95
Languedoc: Carcassonne to Montpellier	£7.99	$11.95
Málaga	£5.99	$8.95
Marseille & Western Provence	£7.99	$11.95
Orkney & Shetland Islands	£5.99	$8.95
Santander & Picos de Europa	£7.99	$11.95
Sardinia: Alghero & the North	£7.99	$11.95
Sardinia: Cagliari & the South	£7.99	$11.95
Seville	£5.99	$8.95
Sicily: Palermo & the Northwest	£7.99	$11.95
Sicily: Catania & the Southeast	£7.99	$11.95
Siena & Southern Tuscany	£7.99	$11.95
Sorrento, Capri & Amalfi Coast	£6.99	$9.95
Skye & Outer Hebrides	£6.99	$9.95
Verona & Lake Garda	£7.99	$11.95

North America	UK RRP	US RRP
Vancouver & Rockies	£8.99	$12.95

Australasia	UK RRP	US RRP
Brisbane & Queensland	£8.99	$12.95
Perth	£7.99	$11.95

For the latest books, e-books and a wealth of travel information, visit us at: www.footprinttravelguides.com.

footprint travelguides.com

Join us on facebook for the latest travel news, product releases, offers and amazing competitions: www.facebook.com/footprintbooks.